CAN SHE BE STOPPED?

CAN
SHE BE
STOPPED?

HILLARY CLINTON

WILL BE THE

NEXT PRESIDENT OF THE

UNITED STATES

UNLESS . . .

JOHN PODHORETZ

CROWN
FORUM
NEW YORK

Crown Forum and Design are registered
trademarks of Random House, Inc.

Library of Congress Cataloging-in-Publication Data

Podhoretz, John.
  Can she be stopped? : Hillary Clinton will be the next president
  unless— / John Podhoretz.—1st ed.
    1. Clinton, Hillary Rodham—Career in politics. 2. Women presidential
  candidates—United States. 3. Presidential candidates—United States.
  4. Presidents—United States—Election—2008. 5. United States—
  Politics and government—2001– 6. United States—Politics and
  government—1993–2001. 7. Political campaigns—United States.
  I. Title.
E887.C55 P63 2006
973.931092—dc22   2006003980

ISBN-13: 978-0-307-33730-6
ISBN-10: 0-307-33730-8

Printed in the United States of America

Design © Level C

10 9 8 7 6 5 4 3 2 1

First Edition

For my sisters, Rachel, Naomi, and Ruthie—
who cannot, should not, and will not be stopped

If you know the enemy and know yourself, you need not fear the result of a hundred battles. If you know yourself but not the enemy, for every victory gained you will also suffer a defeat. If you know neither the enemy nor yourself, you will succumb in every battle.

—Sun Tzu,
The Art of War

CONTENTS

CAN SHE BE STOPPED?

AN OPEN LETTER TO CONSERVATIVES AND REPUBLICANS

The very early hours of Wednesday, November 5, 2008, are going to seem eerily, excitingly, frustratingly familiar to anyone in this country who is older than twelve, has an IQ higher than 100, and has ever watched a TV news program, or read a newspaper, or clicked on a news story. The polls in Alaska will close at midnight Eastern Standard Time, and that will bring to a close the casting of ballots that began twenty-four hours earlier in Dixville Notch, New Hampshire, in the first presidential election since 1952 that will feature neither a sitting president nor a sitting vice president as a candidate for the highest office in the land.

And just as was the case in the two preceding presidential elections, we still won't yet know which of the two—or three—major candidates will be the next president.

For once again, probably after all kinds of confusion caused by yet another set of ill-conceived and politicized exit polls that will have Republicans in a panic and Democrats in a state of unrealistic glee, the electoral map will have fallen into place pretty much as it did on the last two Election Days. States along the Pacific Ocean and the North Atlantic will be colored a solid Democratic blue, while the Southwest, the South, and most of the nation's midsection will shout out in vivid Republican red.

The political operatives crowded together at the huge please-God-let-our-team-win parties in Washington—Democrats packing the Old Post Office, Republicans filling the Ronald Reagan Center—will be awash in anxiety as thousands of unreleased balloons hang far over their heads waiting either to be released in joy or to remain suspended in defeat. For the third election in a row, the vote counts in Ohio, Florida, Michigan, Wisconsin, Missouri, Pennsylvania, and New Hampshire will be inconclusive. Anchormen will be explaining how if the Dems take Florida and Pennsylvania, the Republicans will have to win every other state to record the necessary 270 electoral votes—and then move on to an entirely different set of calculations according to which Republicans need win only Florida and Ohio to get there. After which, a panel made up of blabbermouth pundits, who will be getting punchy and maybe even a tad psycho, will fill some time until the "decision desk" can call another state.

And then, as the tension grows to an almost unbearable level, the toss-up states will begin to tip . . . but which way?

Which way?

If you conservatives and Republicans—you Republican thinkers, strategists, politicians, and voters and you conservative activists, intellectuals, and organizers—can come to a meeting of the minds about the seriousness of the threat facing this country in the next election, you can make sure that the balloons drop on you and not on the other guys. You can forestall and prevent the most frightening and disastrous outcome of that early morning. You can guarantee that the candidate you most dread will not be not standing in front of the west face of the U.S. Capitol alongside Chief Justice John Roberts on January 20, 2009. You can prevent that candidate from being the person who will utter the words spoken by only forty-two other Americans in this nation's history.

Yes, if you do what must be done to ensure that this nation will be safe and secure and economically viable as it enters the second decade of the third millennium, you and your fellow Americans (and the world) will never hear the sentence specified by Article 2, Section 1 of the United States Constitution spoken as follows: "I, Hillary Rodham Clinton, do solemnly swear that I will faithfully execute the office of President of the United States, and will, to the best of my ability, preserve, protect, and defend the Constitution of the United States."

You can end the newest American political dynasty aborning. You can make certain that William Jefferson Clinton does not get to move back into the White House and serve as history's first First Gent. Eight years after his ignominious departure from 1600 Pennsylvania Avenue, amid reports that the White House had been trashed by outgoing staffers and amid general disgust at the extravagant pardons Clinton had been handing out like so many business cards, the man who turned the White House into a fee-for-service hotel and toyed with insecure young women and tortured widows and God knows who else in the nooks and crannies of the West Wing will continue to have to do his wretched business elsewhere.

The flip side of this scenario is also unfortunately true. For if you Republicans don't get real serious real fast, if you don't wise up and settle down and get focused, that *will* be Hillary up there on the podium taking the oath of office from John Roberts. Hillary Rodham Clinton will become the next president of the United States unless you Republicans can find a way to stop her.

And you can.

But to do so, you need to understand just how real the possibility of her victory is and what kind of challenge that poses to you as a party and a movement. You need to come together in recognition of the threat. You need to avoid the temptation that has begun to afflict members of the party's more ideological branches—the temptation to threaten to break off, to secede, to run third-party protest candidacies. That will only get Hillary elected.

———

POLITICIANS AND POLITICAL writers are fond of sports analogies, and when they're looking for one, they usually go straight to football or baseball. Neither is the proper metaphor for what happens in elections. The sport providing the closest analogy is golf. Golf is a game played over a series of days in which a contender must not only compete with others but must also overcome his own natural human tendency to fail—to lose focus, get lazy, ease up, worry himself to death, get cocky and overconfident, or become self-destructive. Usually, the golfer who wins a tournament is the one who makes the fewest unforced errors, the one who gets in his own way the least.

And so it is with politics. Elections in America—and in this case I refer only to contested elections, those increasingly rare events where nobody quite knows on Election Day which of the two leading candidates is going to prevail—are almost never *won*. Indeed, the real trick to winning an election in America isn't to win it. The trick is *not to lose it.* In 2000 and 2004, George W. Bush won the presidency in large measure because he made fewer mistakes than Al ("Let me come across as three different people in three different debates") Gore and John ("I voted for the $87 billion before I voted against it") Kerry.

Now, you can certainly make the case, and I would, that Gore and Kerry made the unforced errors they did because they didn't quite know what they stood for and what message they were trying to get across and so they were superbly well suited to fumfer and blather and trip on their own shoelaces. You can make the case that it was easy for George W. Bush to stick to his rigidly programmed stump speeches, to say the same thing in the same way for months and months and months without going insane, because he knew at his core what he was running for and why selling his message was the best way to get to Washington (or stay in Washington) and do what he thought he needed to do for the country. Or you can make the case that Bush is a boring, programmed robot, lacking the kind of human frailties that might cause a Gore or a Kerry to screw up charmingly.

Whichever side of the argument you take, Bush's two elections prove that *not losing* is a vital part—maybe *the* vital part—of winning. And now, as 2008 approaches, the Republican Party faces a very complicated task. To stop Hillary Clinton, it has to *not lose* to her. To succeed in this aim, Republicans need to start now. You must avoid fights to the death with one another. You know you want to have them. But you can't tear yourselves apart over them. The cost will simply be too high for the country to bear.

This is not to say that disagreements among Republicans and conservatives over matters of policy and conscience are bad and to be avoided. Far from it. The greatest sign of health in the Republican Party is its growing capacity to house people who share the same rough vision of the nation's direction but who have differing views on how to get there. That rough vision, the Republican vision, can be summed up briefly as this: America is and should be a country that rewards individual achievement and hard work, disdains a culture of preferential treatment and group rights, believes in equality of opportunity rather than the equality of result, upholds traditional values, and is dedicated to securing the nation from foreign threats.

Now, do the Republican Party's politicians act in ways

that are always commensurate with this vision? Of course not. They are politicians first and foremost, and most of them are guilty of the same sins that have corrupted elected officials since the dawn of time—especially the sleazy but legal use of public moneys to buy support from voters, reward friends and donors, punish enemies and rivals, and cement their own place in office forever.

In particular, for many rank-and-file Republicans, life would certainly be simpler if the party—the party of traditional values and individual accomplishment—had proved to be more exacting in its management of the Congress in the years since the GOP took it over in 1994 than the party of Big Government was in the forty years preceding it. But that was not to be. Perhaps even hoping that it could have been so was a dangerous illusion. And so many Republicans and movement conservatives, disdainful of Washington and its tendency to turn Puritan reformers into Epicurean revelers, are currently expressing great distress about the behavior of the Washington party—about the rise of creepy lobbyists, the use of Congressional pork, and the prevalence of cronyism.

God knows it would be nice if you could have politics without politicians, but you can't. Politics is a profession, and in general, people behave in nasty and unseemly ways when it comes to keeping their jobs. Politicians are among the reasons why, in his great essay, the novelist E. M. Forster was able to issue only "two cheers for democracy." So as 2008 looms, Republicans and conservatives should be sadder and wiser about politics—sadder because the ideal of a "Republican Revolution" as promulgated in the 1990s proved to be a fantasy, and wiser because it's always better to look at the world through clear and cold eyes rather than rose-colored glasses. And here's what you see when you look through clear and cold eyes: Sometimes, in politics, the best you can do is to play the

Lesser of Two Evils game. You may have to commit yourself to a candidate who is not the most wonderful person you can think of, a candidate who disappoints you and even angers you in many ways—because it's more important to prevent a result you know will be bad news.

Hillary = Bad News.

————————

THE MISCHIEF HILLARY could do in the White House would be far more devastating to the country than anything she and Bill cooked up in the 1990s. I'm not talking about personal peccadilloes, for it seems unquestionable that Hillary's own personal morality resides elsewhere than in the high-rent sewer where her husband's does. And as for financial dirty dealings, she's doubtless learned to keep her nose clean after the Whitewater agony—and the change for the better in the Democratic Party's financial fortunes means she won't have to troll for campaign funds from Chinese Communist agents and grant pardons in exchange for library donations. To that extent, her presidency would be superior to her husband's. Indeed, Bill himself has said she would be a better president than he was—only "in some ways," of course, because in Clinton's own mind, no human being could be better than he at anything. "In some ways," he told an Israel Television anchor in November 2005, "she would be because of what we did together. First, she has the Senate experience I didn't have. Second, she would have had the eight years in the White House. I think she wouldn't make as many mistakes, because, you know, we're older and more mature, and she is far more experienced now in all the relevant ways than I was when I took office. So I think in a way she has the best of both worlds."[1]

Hillary might have the best of both worlds. But America would have the worst of it. We have every reason to believe she would be a far more destructive president than her husband was. Where Bill was a prudent and cautious political player and an ideological vampire, almost always ready and willing to drink deep from the opposition's ideas and command them as though they were his own if it suited his interests, Mrs. Clinton will almost surely use her time in the White House to advance frankly liberal or leftist ideas. At a time when the Left poses a colossal threat to the nation's economic viability and its national security, she will try to run for office from the center but govern from the Left.

If I'm right—and I hope this book will provide ideas and methods that will ensure we need never find out—Hillary's presidency will be the mirror image of the presidency of George W. Bush. There's every reason to believe that Hillary Clinton is to liberalism what George W. Bush was to conservatism—its Trojan Horse, its stealthy way back into power. She's a serious person, a person of conviction, a talented politician, and a tough competitor—just as he was and is.

The current president ran in 2000 as a compassionate conservative, with a greater stress on the compassion than on the conservatism. As president, however, Bush immediately took his stand with the right wing of his party. He found his home, his base, his succor, his sustenance, and, indeed, his vision from the neoconservatives and the conservatives. That's who he really was, as it turned out. Though it is true that Bush dissented from conservative orthodoxy in many ways, chiefly in his refusal to embrace penurious government, he was as right-wing a president as could be imagined in this place and time (as Republicans and conservatives disenchanted with him right now will discover as they begin to examine the likeliest choices to replace him in 2009).

The left-liberal governance of Hillary Clinton would be seen in every aspect of the government. The economic alteration of the nation's course seems easy to predict—tax increases, more government regulation of the economy, a friendly disposition toward the use of the courts by trial lawyers, a war on businesses large and small launched by regulatory agencies in the name of the environment and small investors, and almost certainly a backslide into protectionism (in the name of workers' rights and environmental justice). But those changes pale in comparison to the consequences for the security of the United States and the advance of U.S. interests around the world.

If you are among those who believe, as I do, that the aggressive tactics taken in the War on Terror have helped keep America safe and have so far prevented a number of post-9/11 attacks, then you have every reason to be panicked about the prospect of Hillary's ascension. For there's good reason to believe she would chip away at those aggressive policies and amend them until they are so compromised they will spring as many leaks as a New Orleans levee during a storm surge. And the people she would hire to work for her would seek to reverse whatever aggressive policies they could reverse.

Take, first, the changes in domestic antiterror policy that she would oversee. Though Hillary has generally talked tough on these matters and voted for Bush-sponsored legislation like the Patriot Act, she did vote to sustain a filibuster in December 2005 opposing the act's reauthorization. Her unwillingness to defend this vital law against reckless Democratic efforts to gut it was a hint that her own presidency would probably take up these matters in the form of "cleaning up" domestic antiterror legislation. That "cleanup" effort would, by the time Congress got through with it and she signed it into law, begin erecting new barriers to the good working order of the FBI and CIA and the possibilities of cooperation between them.

The judges she would appoint, all of them left-leaning at

best, would be inclined to use their gavels to rule out of order any and all aggressive efforts at terrorism prevention. And her cabinet officials, drawn from her three decades of friendship with the left-wing majordomos of the United States, would push back against the use of tough and innovative tactics by enforcement agencies and first-responders.

But even those actions would pale beside the changes she would make to the foreign policy of the United States. George W. Bush's aggressive foreign policy—taking the fight to the terrorists and the rogue states and trying to replace Muslim tyrannies with democracies—offers the only real chance to end the endless cycle of Islamofascist terror. But eliminating that foreign policy is the goal that unites every Democrat and leftist. They may disagree on just what exactly should replace it, but replace it they will. That detestation of the Bush foreign policy is the glue that binds the disparate elements of the Democratic coalition—from the Michael Moore crazies who think Bush did it all for oil or for the Saudis or for some other wacko goal to the more sensible Clinton officials who criticize Bush policy because, hell, that's what foreign-policy experts do when they're affiliated with the party out of power.

And where does Hillary stand on all of this? It is true that she has voted for Bush defense budgets and supported the wars in Afghanistan and Iraq. But it is also true that for twenty years before she became a senator, she was committed to a view of the world and America's role in it that was defiantly, even passionately, hostile to a foreign policy that required America to stand tall, defy conventional world opinion, and do what was necessary to secure itself and free the world from tyranny.

Which is the real Hillary? The senator with her eye on the White House, casting votes to keep herself viable, or the activist whose sense of the world remained remarkably unaltered even as her own husband moved to the center? I submit that the senator is the Trojan Horse and the real Hillary is inside, waiting to burst through and alter the course set by George W. Bush. For, in the end, Hillary's almost perfect liberal voting record—she received a 96 rating from the Americans for Democratic Action in 2005—is a more reliable indicator of her ideological purposes than her studied efforts to play a hawk.

Which is why she must be stopped, and you're the only ones who can stop her. But to do that, you first must stop doing something else. You need to stop lying to yourselves. You need to stop having those conversations where you begin to doubt her strength as a candidate. I've heard them. I've participated in them. I've even reveled in them. They're very alluring. After all, you and everyone you know probably despise Hillary Clinton. There's almost nothing about her that appeals to you. You think she stayed in her marriage because she was hungry for unelected power, and that disgusts you. Or you think she stayed in the marriage because she had a kind of addiction to Bill Clinton, which evokes contempt in you, considering all the foul things Bill Clinton did with his incessant philandering.

But *that* Hillary Clinton—the one that was so easy to dislike, even outright hate—won't be the one running for president. As her husband suggested, she's older and wiser and cleverer—and therefore more dangerous. She's shown the most important quality a successful politician can have: She's learned how to adapt. She's learned from her mistakes. And she's even managed to make her mistakes work for her.

When 2008 rolls around, it will have been sixteen years since Hillary first emerged on the American scene. With the possible exceptions of the man who won the Civil War and made his bid for the White House in 1868, the man who defeated the Nazis and went for it in 1952, and the man who costarred in a movie with a chimp named Bonzo and sought the brass ring in 1980, she will be the most famous person ever to run for president.

By the time the 1992 election rolled around, Hillary had already become the best-known would-be First Lady ever— and by the end of the Clinton presidency had achieved a prominence in the role equaled in the course of American history only by Eleanor Roosevelt and Dolley Madison. What's especially interesting about this is that much of her fame was due to mistakes she made, the controversies she created, and the enemies she attracted like flies. She generated unnecessary enmity toward herself before her husband's election because of rude and cold statements about what she clearly took to be the proper liberal role of women.

It happened, basically, the moment America got a look at her on a *60 Minutes* broadcast on the eve of the New Hampshire primary in which she and Bill sat together to answer Gennifer Flowers's charge that she had engaged in a twelve-year affair with the presidential hopeful. It was on this occasion that the then-unknown Hillary Clinton angrily and contemptuously declared she wasn't "standing by my man, like Tammy Wynette." The remark was a reference to a twenty-four-year-old country-music song, and it was significant because everybody got the message: Hillary Clinton may have moved to the South and been the wife of a Southern Democratic governor, but she was a Northern liberal through and through.

Nothing wrong with being a Northern liberal—hey, I'm married to one—but there was something wrong about a would-be First Lady becoming a controversial character right off the bat. And she just couldn't help herself, somehow; she stepped in it yet again only a few weeks after the Tammy Wynette moment, when she proudly told reporters that she had pursued a profession rather than being a housewife. It was, to put it mildly, unwise for her to act as though what she did was far more important and difficult than what homemakers and other nonprofessional women did.

Those personal mistakes were compounded in the first two years of Bill Clinton's presidency by the grave political mistake she made as First Lady in designing and championing a disastrously statist overhaul of the nation's health care practices. So having become a lightning rod for being a caricature of a women's libber during the campaign, Hillary then became a caricature of a clueless and dogmatic leftist as a result of her bungled health care plan.

The final element of her early fame was intertwined with the mistakes she had made in Arkansas and continued to make in Washington in regard to some suspicious financial transactions during her time as a prominent young politician's wife. The shadow cast over her by her surprising ability to earn a 10,000 percent profit on a cattle-futures deal when she had never before dealt in futures offered a rather more ambiguous picture of the First Lady than you would have guessed from the air of moral superiority she bore as conspicuously as the bright pink suit in which she appeared at a press conference inside the White House to explain her lucky cattle score.

The first sign that Hillary Clinton might indeed be a formidable political force on her own was when she quieted down and put herself in a box in 1996 so that her husband could get reelected. She understood that the controversies she provoked were bad for him, and rather than standing her ground proudly, she shut her yapper.

She opened it in a significant way only once more before she ran for the Senate in New York—when in the week that Monica Lewinsky's name first surfaced in 1998, she went on the *Today* show and declared that a "vast right-wing conspiracy" had come into existence to force her husband to accept oral sex and phone sex from an unpaid twenty-one-year-old intern.

It turned out that silence served her well—so well, in fact, that she decided to make it an integral part of her own political strategy when she ran for the U.S. Senate in New York State in 1999 and 2000. She spent much of the first year in her two-year campaign on what she called a "listening tour" of the Empire State's sixty-two counties. In other words, she wasn't going to say anything on the record, would be giving no speeches, and wouldn't sit for interviews about the race. She was just going to "listen" instead.

This, again, demonstrated the political smarts that Hillary had developed during the Clinton presidency. She was not yet quite skilled enough to wing it on the campaign trail with a huge press corps hanging on her every word. One bad mistake and she might be toast. So the woman who became famous for sticking her foot in her mouth glided into the Senate by saying and doing almost nothing.

And by keeping quiet throughout her Senate tenure, Hillary Clinton helped squelch the fires of the rage against her, because she has added little fuel to them. During the Bush presidency, Hillary Clinton has been serving as the junior senator from New York, careful to avoid making waves, casting reliably liberal Democratic votes, and yet cultivating a reputation as a centrist largely because she voted to authorize the use of force in the war against Saddam and has supported every defense appropriation since.

The tale told about Hillary Clinton's tenure in the Senate is that she is just so very, very "hardworking." It's hard to know what that actually means, since the work of a senator is to sit around listening to people blather and take lots of meetings, but it's been the standard line about her—and what's even more interesting is that the line has been peddled most frequently not by Hillary's fellow Democrats but by Republicans like John McCain and Lindsey Graham.

In ways large and small, then, the Clinton project of this decade has been to soften and becalm the image of the 1990s virago who was the subject of comedian Jeff Foxworthy's immortal crack, "If you have nothing nice to say, you must be talking about Hillary Clinton." And truth to tell, Hillary is nothing if not a survivor, and she's been around long enough to seem like a piece of political-cultural furniture, heavy and present and in your living room whether you like it or not.

That much became evident in 2002, with the publication of her astoundingly uninformative and uninspired memoir, *Living History*. Whatever its weaknesses as a work of literature—and suffice it to say it has no strengths as a work of literature—*Living History* was an astounding success. Conservatives scoffed when her publishing house paid $8 million for the book, which led one of the biggest scoffers, the TV host–pundit Tucker Carlson, to say he'd eat his shoe if *Living History* sold 1 million copies. Carlson's ingestion of a cake in the shape of a shoe was a landmark moment—including for skeptics in her own political camp—because it demonstrated that Hillary Clinton really did possess mass appeal on her own.

The book's success cemented the notion among Democrats in particular that she might be their savior from the hard-charging Bush in 2004—and when she wisely decided not even to dip her tippy-toe into the waters of that maelstrom, it made her the prohibitive frontrunner for her own party's nomination in four years' time.

Her status as a frontrunner and her access to her husband's fundraising machine mean that Hillary Clinton begins the presidential-campaign cycle roughly where Bush did in 1999—so far ahead in terms of money-raising abilities that a whole bunch of other prospective candidates may just decide not even to give it a shot.

Actually, she's probably in a far stronger position than Bush was. She is also using her Senate reelection bid in New York to begin loading up her bank account. Hillary will face no significant opposition, and yet will probably raise between

$50 and $100 million before Election Day 2006. By February 2006, according to press reports, she had already banked $17.5 million. Federal election law will allow her to transfer the unused money from that Senate campaign into her presidential coffers. This suggests that Hillary will be in a position to break through the $40 million primary campaign-spending limit more than a year earlier than Bush did, and he was the first candidate in the modern era ever to decide to run a primary campaign entirely with private funds.* By 2007, she will be the 800-pound gorilla of the coming election.

The only way to deal with an enemy is to take that enemy seriously, to respect the enemy's strengths, to understand the enemy's virtues. And you can't shake off your worry by thinking dismissive thoughts. You need to give up on attractive theories that tell you Hillary Clinton is *not* a strong candidate for president. You need to restrain yourself from being seduced by a few ideas that are already being bandied about to suggest that she is a weak contender who will be easy to defeat. These seductive ideas come from decades of received political wisdom, and they all seem to rule Hillary Clinton out of order and unable to reach the Oval Office. Now, I would never disagree with the contention that the best guide to how politicians will win in the future is the close study of how other politicians have won and lost in the past. But in every successful presidential campaign, the candidate and his team also figure out a new way to win and upset the conventional wisdom that prevailed before them.

Nobody before 1988 thought a patrician vice president could successfully peddle a populist message against a candi-

---

* By breaking the spending limit, Bush was unable to collect federal matching funds. In effect, then, he was betting that he could raise more than $80 million, which he did both elections—more than $100 million each in 2000 and 2004.

date raised by poor immigrants from Greece, but George Bush the Elder did. Nobody before 1992 thought it would be a good idea for a candidate from the South to pick a vice presidential candidate from the same region—but it worked when Clinton chose Gore. Nobody before 2000 thought that the son of a failed president could make it to the Oval Office, but George Bush the Younger did. Nobody before 2004 thought that a presidential election could be won by milking a candidate's own base rather than moving toward the center for votes—and yet that's how George W. Bush succeeded in scoring 62 million ballots with his name on them.

And yet political thinkers and watchers are sorely tempted to believe in the conventional wisdom they have come to know so well, because without it, what do they actually know, really? Which is why it's essential to examine the conventional wisdom and challenge its assumptions.

———————

"DEPEND UPON IT, SIR," said Dr. Johnson, "when a man knows he is to be hanged in a fortnight, it concentrates his mind wonderfully." Hillary's election should be concentrating the minds of Republicans and conservatives wonderfully. But it isn't yet. And if we're not careful, the disappointment many of you feel with the state of your party will translate into an exhilarating but potentially suicidal journey as the primary season gets under way in earnest in 2007. The road you should travel, the path you should take, is the one marked "Danger: Hillary Approaching." But there are nascent signs that you may take another road, a road into the interior of the Republican Party itself. Many on the right will want to use the primary to lead the GOP and the country into some very dangerous territory—ideological purity.

Occasionally in politics, a small but influential caucus of idealists decides that what its party really needs is a Purification

Ritual. To stress the importance of ideological purity, the caucus will stage a protest candidacy against a mainstream politician and the political party that chooses him, because the party and the politician have betrayed the caucus's highest ideals.

The conservative movement that undergirds the Republican Party is especially fond of threatening the GOP with a Purification Ritual on every matter under the sun. Even Ronald Reagan's presidency wasn't good enough for many conservatives, who continually declared themselves good and ready to form a third party whose sole purpose would be to divide the GOP—to injure the party and prevent its candidates from winning elections. This was, presumably, a form of tough love, an effort to force change on a recalcitrant party. Or at least that's what the Purifiers usually say. But in fact they are doing what insurgencies always do—engaging in destruction and calling it revolution.

The GOP's conservative base is very susceptible to the temptation to Purify, because even though the Republican Party and the conservative movement are enemies of the Left's utopian politics, we are often guilty of indulging in our own form of utopianism when it comes to politics and politicians. We cannot bear it if they don't devote themselves to all our policy hopes and wishes, and we experience a yearning to punish them for their heterodoxy. That's where the Purification Ritual comes in.

Now, it's certainly the case that the Purifiers exist in both parties. The Democratic Party has been wounded by the Ritual as well. In 1948, two Purification candidates—radical leftist Henry Wallace and Southern segregationist Strom Thurmond—ran against Harry Truman and nearly handed the election to Republican Thomas Dewey. Twenty years later, George Wallace took direction from Thurmond's racist playbook and stole Southern votes away from Lyndon Johnson in 1968. And, of course, in 2000, Ralph Nader—a Henry

Wallace for the new millennium—took a small but crucial bite out of Al Gore.

But in recent decades the GOP has been subjected to Purification Rituals far more frequently than the Democrats—and at far greater cost, at least in 1992. The GOP's Purification Temptation first surfaced in a realm that no longer even exists on our political spectrum—in the left wing of the GOP. In 1972, a Republican congressman named Paul McCloskey decided to run as a third-party candidate against Richard Nixon, who was up for reelection. McCloskey's intent was not to win but rather to speak as the voice of his party's liberal conscience on foreign policy. Since there was little difference between McCloskey and Democratic candidate George McGovern—and since neither his nor McGovern's message had much appeal—McCloskey did Nixon no damage.

In 1980, another liberal Republican, Congressman John Anderson of Illinois, tried to throw a monkey wrench into the electoral proceedings by staging a third-party assault on Ronald Reagan from the left. He too was unsuccessful, since Reagan won an absolute majority with 51 percent of the vote. (Anderson actually took some votes away from Democrat Jimmy Carter.)

Despite their failure, the liberal Republican candidates planted a seed that came to fruition in 1992—first in the primaries, when the Neanderthal commentator Pat Buchanan became the vehicle for far-right-wing anger with George Bush the Elder, and then when the wacko billionaire H. Ross Perot made his Sherman's March through Republican strongholds in the November election. Perot, who had never run for office and was all but unknown when 1992 began, scored an amazing 19 percent of the vote and basically gave the presidency to Bill Clinton. Four years later, Perot did it again, getting 8 percent of the vote. And while it's doubtful that Republican Bob Dole could have bested the resurgent incumbent Clinton under any circumstances, the fact is that if you add Dole's and Perot's vote total, together they beat the Man from Hope by a few hundred thousand.

Though neither Perot nor Buchanan was an ideal vehicle for the voter who cast his lot with the protest—since one was nutty and the other was noxious—there's no question why the protest was being staged and for what purpose. Daddy Bush had raised taxes when he had said he wouldn't, and had signed three major pieces of big-government legislation when he had said he would pursue smaller government. Bob Dole was the Washington Establishment Republican par excellence, uncomfortable with any issue that moved and excited voters. Perot was not an ideological Purifier—he talked too much about getting under the hood and seeing what was wrong with the engine, as though a representative government were a machine and not an ingathering of fallen men and women—but he provided an outlet for the frustration of those disappointed by the Republicans.

Lovely. There's nothing like casting a ballot for someone who can never win to make you feel like Don Quixote, nobly (if crazily) tilting at windmills. But this is no time for Republicans and conservatives to be quixotic. You have to get over the hunger to seek exile and isolation for those fellow Republicans with whom you disagree. In this coming election, it is vital for the nation's future that you resist the siren song of Purification. You must not hold ideological purity more dear than partisan victory in the coming two years.

Yes, it's time to fight, but it's not time to fight one another. It's time, instead, to start picking the right fights. I'm talking about fights with the liberal Left that will rally your voters, inspire your donors, and offer the Democrats a temptation of their own—the temptation they have been courting for years now. You want them to redirect their own politics far off to the left, to take a leap off a cliff and into the swirling rapids of hatred and rage at all things Republican and conservative.

You want Democrats to suffer the fate they suffered the last time they ran a presidential candidate following a two-term Republican president. That was Michael Dukakis in 1988, who lost the election by 8 points (54–46). Now, Hillary Clinton is not Michael Dukakis, and the nature of the current American electorate makes it almost impossible for the 2008 election to feature a victory that sizable by either side. But it is conceivable, if you Republicans and conservatives put your minds to it, that you could do things in the coming two years that would help push the Democratic Party away from the more electable Hillary into the arms of a more frankly leftist candidate.

That candidate would probably be Howard Dean—yes, Howard Dean, the man who shouted "yeeargh" like a crazed banshee, the man who later became chairman of the Democratic National Committee. Certainly, Dean would be a pleasure for the GOP to run against, but it need not be he. Al Gore—the new Al Gore, the crazy and hysterical Al Gore, the Al Gore who no longer speaks as though he had been anesthetized but rather like someone in dire need of Librium, the Al Gore who likens those who dare to criticize him on talk radio and the Internet to Hitler's brownshirts— would do just fine too. So would Wisconsin senator Russ Feingold, a classic up-from-academia American leftist. John Kerry has also been moving steadily left in hopes of finding solid ground for his 2008 bid. Or it could be someone we've never even thought of, the way nobody had even thought of Howard Dean as suitable for much more than taking a drive between Montpelier and Brattleboro in early 2002.

The point is that Republicans should act in ways that will drive Democrats so batty they will strengthen the hand of the left-wing rump that might consider Hillary a centrist sellout, allowing whatever Republican candidate who shows up in November 2008 to waltz away with the election.

I grant you this is neither probable nor likely. Mark

Blumenthal, a Democratic pollster and blogger, points out that despite virulent anti-Hillary rhetoric on some left-wing sites in 2005, she maintained a favorable rating among Democrats somewhere between 79 and 84 percent.[2] But it is conceivable—if you are clever enough and determined enough to make it happen. And even if you don't succeed at that delicious goal, the act of attempting it may force Hillary herself to move so far to the left to secure the Democratic nomination that she will be unelectable by the time the two party conventions are over at the end of August. And even if *that* doesn't happen, doing what is necessary to hold your own party together is the only way she *can* be stopped.

There is more than mere pragmatism in this for you. Coming together in recognition of a common enemy is powerful binding glue for a party and a political movement, even if they feel themselves to be in the doldrums and spoiling for an internecine battle. Many Republicans and conservatives feel that their party and their movement have become strange victims of their own successes—that the Bush triumphs in fighting the war against Islamic radicalism have been obscured by the difficulty of finishing the job in Iraq, and that the Republican takeover of Congress has not led to a greater devolution of power to the individual but rather to an unhealthy fondness for feeding its friends from the public teat. But whatever weaknesses and sins have beset the Republicans and the Right, they are as nothing compared with what Hillary Rodham Clinton might be in a position to do if she wins the presidency, and you know that down to the root.

This isn't about the visceral personal dislike many on the right have for Hillary Clinton. This is about the future of the country, and what the country needs now is for the Right to stop her. For parties and movements to lead and to succeed, they need missions. Well, this is the mission, and this is your moment. Let's get to it. Now.

Part I

WHY, IN SPITE OF EVERYTHING, HILLARY CAN BE ELECTED PRESIDENT

Chapter 1

YES, SHE HAS "HIGH NEGATIVES"— AND THEY MIGHT EVEN HELP HER

Hillary will begin her race with a startlingly large number of Americans holding a negative opinion of her—somewhere around 40 percent. Lee Atwater, the late Republican political operative who helped develop some of the most potent anticandidate techniques—the ones we call "negative campaigning"—once said that if you could push an office-seeker's negative number above 40 percent, there would be no way that office-seeker could win his race.

Since Hillary starts out there, at 40 percent, it would take very little change for her to reach the level beyond which she simply couldn't prevail in a national election. That has led some very intelligent Republicans and conservatives to believe that she cannot prevail in a national election.

It's a tempting thought for those who don't want Hillary to be president—the idea that the injuries she did to her own reputation in the 1990s will make it impossible for her to rise any higher than she already has. It's one thing to win an election as senator from New York, a state with a 3-to-1 Democratic advantage in registration, a blue state that gets bluer and bluer by the day. It's quite another to win in a nation where twice as many people say they're "conservative" as say they're "liberal." The country hasn't forgotten who

Hillary is, and if people have forgotten, they'll quickly remember once they've been reminded.

In fact, according to this analysis, she might be easier to
beat than any other Democrat precisely because she finds
herself at the starting gate with so many people actively dis-
liking her, even hating her. Democrats would therefore be
handing Republicans a great gift by nominating Hillary, because it wouldn't require much energy or effort to ensure
that tens of millions of Americans hold an unfavorable opinion of her in 2008. This analysis is tempting, reassuring, and
promising. It is also wrong.

In previous decades, Hillary's negatives would have torpe-
doed her candidacy. But there have been major changes in
the past fifteen years that have altered the rules of American
politics. The changes have to do with the way Americans
think about politics, where Americans place themselves on
the political spectrum, the increasing bitterness between the
two parties, and the rallying effect now caused when a partisan politician becomes a target for the other side.

From 1980 to 2004, the number of Americans willing
to identify themselves as Republicans grew by 25 percent,
while the number of self-identified Democrats shrank by
20 percent. This collective realization has had profound political consequences. For one thing, it means we have now
basically reached parity between the two parties, with passionate partisans on each side counting for somewhere between 35 and 40 percent of the vote. These are hard-core
voters who, at least for the foreseeable future, will never,
ever cast a vote for the other side.

In an election that swings to the Democrat, as was the
case in 1996, the number of voters who say they are Democrats in exit polls and other data will be a tad higher than
the Republican number, 38 to 36. In 2004, with the Republican Bush prevailing, the GOP number was a little higher
than the Democratic number.

In practical terms, the rise of party parity helped bring down the curtain on the Democratic era on Capitol Hill. Four decades in which Democrats were in charge of both chambers of the American legislature (with the exception of Ronald Reagan's first six years in office) came to an ignominious end in 1994—and only the weird defection of a liberal Republican senator in 2001 allowed the Senate to revert to Democratic control for about seventeen months before the 2002 election handed the chamber back to the GOP.

This all sounds like fantastic news for the GOP, no? The country becomes more and more Republican, the party takes over the legislature and then the presidency and does pretty well at the state and local levels as well. Why, then, should there be worry about the probable competition from the most controversial woman in America?

Well, here's the bitter irony. The fact that the country has become more Republican as a result of the Clinton era may end up helping Hillary where the high-negatives problem is concerned. Polarization makes her elevation to the top of her party's heap more, not less, likely—and could get her elected.

In order to explain how this is true, we need to go back and talk about how political parity came to be and the role played by the Clintons in hastening its arrival.

———————

LEE ATWATER CAME UP with his 40 percent formula during the 1980s, when far more Americans said they were Democrats than said they were Republicans—Democrats remained around 40 percent, while Republicans scored anywhere between 25 and 30 percent in the Harris poll.[1] Given that statistic, it seemed an insuperable challenge for Republicans to win office anywhere but in solid GOP states. Atwater and others figured out how to break the Democratic logjam, especially in the South—a region that maintained a significant

Democratic advantage in party registration even as Democratic voters turned out in droves both for Richard Nixon in 1972 and for Ronald Reagan in 1980 and 1984.

Atwater and the Atwaterites knew that while voters were more likely to call themselves Democrats and to hold Democratic Party registration, they were also far more likely to describe themselves as conservative than liberal—according to the Harris poll, 37 percent conservative to 17 percent liberal in 1985.[2] Though Republican strategists could not depend on a solid bloc of Republican voters that would bring their candidates within striking distance, they could peel voters away from the Democrat by going after him not because of his party affiliation but because of his views.

The goal of the GOP in the 1980s was to demonstrate to Democratic voters that there was a huge gulf between their values and interests and those of the elite Democrats who ran for office. If they could succeed at that task, they could get those voters to take a good look at the Republican candidate instead, for whom they would once never have voted. As a result, successful Republican campaigns outside GOP-dominated states focused on a candidate individually and specifically. They looked for symbolic ways to reveal how out-of-step he was with ordinary voters.

It wasn't hard to do, because the nation's liberal elite was, at the time, committed to a series of interlocking ideas that were actually anathema to many of the members of the old FDR-era voting bloc.

Liberals opposed taking a tough stance against Communism abroad and spoke of the United States as bearing equal responsibility for the tensions of the Cold War, while most Americans believed America was the good guy and the Soviet Union the villain. Liberals fought against the Vietnam War in a fashion that either belittled or slandered the boys fighting and dying there, when those boys were the sons of working-class people who tended to vote Democratic.

And, of course, there was abortion. In 1972, the Democratic Party candidate, George McGovern, said flatly, "You can't just let anybody walk in and request an abortion," and both of his vice presidential nominees (the quickly bounced Thomas Eagleton and his replacement, Sargent Shriver) were passionately pro-life. And while the 1976 Democratic Party platform opposed a constitutional amendment to overturn *Roe v. Wade,* Jimmy Carter said repeatedly during the campaign that he was "pro-life." This reflected the reality of the Democratic coalition at the time, which was a mixture of the social liberals of the 1960s who had taken over the party's governing structure and the far more socially conservative (primarily Catholic) urban constituencies that helped form the party's voting base.

By 1984, however, any circumspection or division in the Democratic Party's view of abortion had vanished, and references in the Republican Party platform to differences of opinion about abortion had vanished as well. The GOP had become the pro-life party, pure and simple, the Democrats the spokespersons for abortion on demand. Indeed, over time, every major Democratic figure with pro-life views—from House Majority Leader Dick Gephardt to Senator Ted Kennedy—abandoned them, even though many traditional Democratic voters viewed abortion as murder, plain and simple.

A fascinating alliance of Catholics and Protestants—orthodox followers of the Pope and evangelicals, two groups who in a previous era would have hated each other and been at war with each other—instead entered into a meeting of the minds. The result was a movement unlike any the United States had ever seen—a movement that has been extraordinarily unsuccessful at its primary aim, the elimination of abortion, and vastly more successful at its secondary aim, the self-conscious introduction of traditionalist moral views into the American political conversation.

And it was precisely American tradition that was most profoundly under liberal elite attack in the 1970s and 1980s. The young Hillary Rodham herself gave voice to this attack in the notorious commencement address she delivered upon her graduation from Wellesley College in 1969, when she said that people of her generation were "searching for more immediate, ecstatic and penetrating modes of living" than the conventions of American society would grant them.[3]

The traditional American home was, according to the radical rhetoric that had infected the world of left-liberalism, little more than a prison for women and a stifling atmosphere for children. This was the subject of Hillary's own limited academic work. Children might need to be freed from "the empire of the father," as she wrote in a November 1973 *Harvard Educational Review* article advocating a radical definition of "children's rights." She referred to children as "child citizens" and compared the restricted rights of childhood in a family setting to "marriage, slavery and the Indian reservation system."[4] Her use of the word *marriage* in that sentence indicated as well that she believed the traditional role of wife and mother was tantamount to being a slave or a Native American forced into a desolate earthscape.

Ordinary voters were obsessed by their fear of criminals, while the liberal elite seemed to devote its sympathy to the criminals themselves. Case in point: law student Hillary Rodham, who worked on behalf of the violent revolutionary group the Black Panthers during her time at Yale Law School. Ordinary voters believed numerical quotas giving preferential treatment to minorities were grotesquely unfair, while the liberal elites were insistent on them. Ordinary voters loved the military and had family members who fought for the country in Vietnam. The liberal elite was hostile to the military and didn't know a soul who had fought there (except for the ones who knew John Kerry). Ordinary voters liked school prayer and the Pledge of Allegiance. The liberal elite was almost obsessive in its efforts to do away with both. Ordinary voters were profoundly confused by abortion, but certainly seemed to believe that teenage girls shouldn't be able to get one without their parents knowing about it. Liberals insisted on an absolute right to an abortion, in perfect secrecy, without parental consent.

On and on it went, down the line. Polls would show vast public support for one policy or another that elite liberal opinion simply asserted was wrongheaded—and presumed that those who held such views were (as one *Washington Post* reporter said of members of the Christian Right) "uneducated and easy to command."[5] Ordinary Americans felt their way of life threatened and their opinions discounted by the nation's opinion leaders, even though in both cases the ordinary folk and the opinion leaders were at this point more likely to share the same Democratic political affiliation.

This divide is what gave rise to the notorious commercials that converted the word *liberal* into a horrifying pejorative, spat out of the mouth of an unseen narrator with the same sort of contempt with which you might say "child molester."

It worked. Atwater and others used the antiliberal technique brilliantly in presidential campaigns and then, slowly but surely, in senatorial, congressional, and gubernatorial elections. And over time, those once-Democratic voters became unconscious Republican fellow travelers, generally preferring GOP candidates over Democrats but still not quite ready to get off the donkey and climb aboard the elephant. They moved instead into the independent category. And there was indeed a history-altering independent hiccup in 1992, when a huge mass of them—22 million—expressed their anger with the GOP and their disgust with the Democrats by voting for the incoherent, no-nonsense, billionaire flake Ross Perot.

Only two years later, in 1994, the jig was up. The Perot

voter basically threw in the towel—and threw in his lot with the GOP. The result was the takeover of Congress by the GOP for the first time in forty years in one of the most lopsided legislative elections in American history.

What happened? The Clintons happened. The speed of the shift toward the GOP, which began in earnest in 1980 and slowed down during the recession of 1990–91, was hastened by the advent of the Clintons on the national scene. Between 1992 and 1994, the Clintons did so many things in so many ways to appall and disgust their fellow Americans—both ideologically and personally—that an astonishing number of them decided to climb aboard the elephant and stay there. In 1994, the political realignment that had been in the works for twenty years finally took root—and for that, Republicans have Bill and Hillary Clinton to thank.

Having won an election with 43 percent of the vote—meaning that 57 percent of the electorate voted against him—Clinton fundamentally misread the politics of his moment. He ran as a moderate Democrat but then chose to govern, for the most part, as a liberal. Having campaigned on cutting taxes, he raised them. Having promised to reform health care, he instead proposed a massive government takeover of health care. Having sounded a cautionary note on abortion, which he said should be "safe, legal and rare," he made sure the first act of his presidency was rescinding the so-called Mexico City rule, which forbade the use of American aid money for overseas abortions. In a nation where somewhere between 35 and 49 percent of households kept a gun on the premises,[6] Bill and Hillary Clinton both expressed the view that gun ownership needed to be controlled through a series of regulations and new laws. Bill pushed for and signed the "Brady Bill," restricting gun purchases.

Clinton may have been a Southern governor with a Southern accent, but he governed like the Georgetown and Yale grad he also was. When the American people said they wanted somebody to fix health care, what they meant was that they couldn't stand their HMOs. They didn't want the U.S. government to set up giant HMOs that would be even less responsive to them—the idea that was the centerpiece of Hillary's key contribution to the public-policy debate in the 1990s.

Clinton's conduct in office seemed to be proof positive that all those nasty things Republican fellow travelers had been hearing from Republican political campaigns about Democrats and the Democratic Party were true. The Democrats were a bunch of liberals, and they wanted to do things to America that voters did not want done.

Those were the specific policy decisions that hurt Clinton terribly and set up an election in 1994 from which the Republican Party emerged in the strongest position it had held in Washington in forty years. But it was not merely the political conduct of Bill Clinton that helped cement the GOP advantage in 1994. There was the intangible set of cultural messages that emanated from his White House, from him personally, and—equally important—from his wife.

AS I'VE SAID, Hillary Clinton was basically introduced to the American people in 1992 during that *60 Minutes* interview that dealt with the exposure of her husband's affair with Gennifer Flowers.* This was the make-or-break moment of his political life, and he would not have gotten through it successfully without Hillary sitting beside him. There had never been anything like it before, just as there had never

---

* Clinton fans spent most of the 1990s claiming there was no evidence for this affair, but Clinton admitted it under oath in 1998.

been a presidential candidate's wife like Hillary before—a career woman who was actually her family's breadwinner with her own history of political activism separate from her husband's, someone who had refused to take her husband's name until it became politically necessary for him. Some of that was bound to rankle, if only because of the novelty of her role.

But during the interview, what America saw was a political wife protecting the political future of her husband. She sat beside him as he acknowledged there had been "problems in our marriage," and even declared herself sorry for the women who had been pursued by the press over the years, because they were innocent, as was he. As he denied flatly that he had dallied with Flowers, Hillary gave him the cover he needed to escape from a career-killing blow.

This was perhaps the most embarrassing position a political spouse had ever been put in—to talk about her husband's extracurricular activities on the highest-rated show on national television. How could one not feel for Hillary in that position? But whatever emotion it was she evoked during that interview, it wasn't sympathy. Through her body language and the shrill, insistent tone in her voice, Hillary scorned any sympathy that she might have received. And she didn't receive it, from either the Left or the Right. The Left thought she showed toughness and resolve. The Right . . . well, the Right was disgusted by the spectacle of a faithless marriage being held up as an equivalent to all marriages. "There isn't a person watching this," said Hillary, "who would feel comfortable sitting here on this couch detailing everything that ever went on in life or their marriage."[7]

This was a remarkable thing to say, not because it wasn't true but because it was Hillary telling America that her marriage wasn't any different from anybody else's. Indeed, she implied it might even have been better in some way: "I'm sitting here because I love him, and I honor what we've been through together. And you know, if that's not enough for people, then heck, don't vote for him."

This was no Pat Nixon or Mamie Eisenhower—a quiet political wife. Nor was she Barbara Bush, the hard-as-nails First Lady who was, nonetheless, still a lady. Hillary was tough all right, but her toughness had a self-congratulatory quality to it. She was both putting herself before the country to soften its judgment of her husband and insisting that neither of them could actually be judged for their conduct.

But the moment that really gave birth to the Right's passionate detestation for Hillary Clinton was her seemingly throwaway remark "I'm not sitting here—some little woman standing by my man, like Tammy Wynette." She spat the words out, as though the traditional role reflected in the song were beneath contempt. The sick irony, of course, was that she was doing Tammy Wynette one better. She was standing *in front of* her man like a protective vest, shielding him from the ill opinion of Americans by claiming resolutely that he was being slandered by an attack machine using Gennifer Flowers as its weapon (when, as we now know, Flowers's allegations were true).

You could spend an entire book analyzing those few words and what they expressed, unconsciously or not so unconsciously—the self-loathing, loathing of Bill Clinton, loathing of other women, love of herself, and love of her husband. But America didn't need to do much analyzing. Hillary Hatred sprang to life at that moment. Whatever her marriage was, and is, it certainly did not look like the kind of union traditionalists liked or appreciated. Forget for a moment the issue of infidelity, which really is a private matter between the two of them (after all, if they chose to continue a marriage despite the unfaithfulness of one of the parties, that's their business). What offended was the suggestion that Hillary and Bill formed a new kind of power couple—a governor who made policy while his litigator wife brung home the bacon. And that, moreover, this new kind of coupledom ought to be given a special pass because there was something so fresh and so noble about it.

Only a few weeks after the Tammy Wynette moment, when confronted by a difficult question raised by rival candidate Jerry Brown about a savings-and-loan issue her law firm had sought to negotiate with her husband's Little Rock government, Hillary turned the whole thing into a feminist cri de coeur. "I suppose I could have stayed home, baked cookies and had teas," she said in exasperation, "but what I decided was to fulfill my profession." This remark was really nothing more than a dodge, a way to avoid the ethics question raised by Jerry Brown. She was using high dudgeon as an expedient political tool, something the two of them would do again and again throughout Clinton's ethically compromised presidency. It worked, in a sense, because she never really had to address the underlying issue Brown had raised.

———————

AND PRECISELY BECAUSE she and Bill did have a new kind of marriage, they seemed determined at times to suggest that there should be new rules governing them. Bill said he would consider appointing Hillary to his cabinet, and also said that people should vote for him because with Hillary it would be "buy one, get one free." Aside from the fact that a federal law (written after John Kennedy appointed his brother as attorney general) prohibited her holding a cabinet position, this was most assuredly the first time a person running for president suggested he would be do a better job with policy and ideas because his wife was going to contribute to them.

All the contradictions of power feminism were present in this unusual coupling. Hillary displayed the self-righteous anger that seemed designed to intimidate people into taking her seriously but was entirely inappropriate. She was someone who had been taken seriously her entire life—delivering a lecture to her elders at that commencement ceremony in 1969, helping prepare the terms of impeachment for Richard Nixon while an aide on Capitol Hill in 1974, working as a law professor before she was thirty, and becoming a partner in a powerful Little Rock law firm at the age of thirty-one. She had had an easy path, in part owing to the rise of feminism. The angry, cold demeanor seemed unnecessary. And since it was unnecessary, it seemed to be merely the expression of the feminist faith in the idea that women had forever been subject to terrible mistreatment. At the same time, it looked as though she wanted all the prerogatives of the traditional political wife as well. Which is to say, she wanted to be the power behind the throne because of her husband's political success—only she was not content to sit behind the throne she had not been elected to occupy, but wanted to share it as a matter of noblesse oblige.

Criticize her feminist leanings, and you were insulting a politician's wife. Call her a politician's wife, and you were insulting the power lawyer. Hillary sought, indeed demanded, exemption from all boundaries she found inconvenient and behaved as though anyone who dared question her exempt status was doing so out of ill motive.

Her demeanor and conduct, along with her husband's political zigzagging and spinning, were potent fuel for a surging conservative media movement that focused on both Clintons like a laser beam, zapping them and broadcasting the news about their badness to an audience far larger than anybody imagined.

It was the rise of this conservative media, more than anything else, that gave the universe of newly minted Republicans a sense of community, a sense that they were among millions of others who felt as they did. That sense of community strengthened and deepened their commitment to the GOP, whereas in prior decades the lack of a conservative media to strengthen the backbone of the ordinary voter might have led some of them to backslide into the Democratic fold.

So they grew together, Hillary Clinton and Rush Limbaugh. As the Clinton candidacy threaded the needle of American politics and eked out a victory in 1992 and then stumbled and bumbled along in 1993 and 1994, it seemed that every word out of Hillary Clinton's mouth, every action she took, and every comment made in praise of her by her supporters were designed to outrage and enrage traditionalist America.

HILLARY HATRED IS ONE of the reasons that, between the election in 1992 and the one in 1994, longtime GOP fellow travelers at last admitted to themselves that they were Republicans, and what's more, that they were Republicans to the core.

Once people achieve partisan consciousness, they are like converts to a faith or newly minted members of a tribe. They no longer need to be convinced to vote, or how to vote, or whom to vote for. They know. And they know, in large measure, because they know whom they don't want to hold office. The other party is the Other. Its politicians are the Bad Guys—not Osama bin Laden bad guys, more like the New York Yankees are to Boston Red Sox fans.

For instance, Republicans who didn't know very much about John Kerry didn't need much convincing in the spring of 2004 that he was a Bad Guy—and were very much open to every conceivable bit of information that might be added to the overall indictment of his character, his political record, his career, even his marital choices. Republicans believed

Kerry was a flip-flopper. They also believed he was a danger-ous liberal ideologue—even though you can't quite believe both things at the same time and still be consistent.

By the time Election Day rolled around, John Kerry had earned the solid disgust of an enormous portion of the Ameri-can electorate, despite the fact that most of them hadn't heard of him until the beginning of the year. He was disliked about as much as Hillary.

And that's the key point. Add the current polarized envi-ronment—when Democrats can say with a serious face that George W. Bush is the worst president in the nation's history and Republicans can say Democrats are effectively working as the silent partners of the Iraqi terrorist insurgency—to the incredible velocity with which news travels and new stories are circulated by cable news, talk radio, and the Internet, and a nobody can become a hated villain in no time.

What this means, in turn, is that *any* candidate who be-comes his or her party's nominee in the spring of 2008 will be viewed very, very negatively by 35 to 40 percent of the na-tion's electorate. That would be true even of the fabled John McCain, who imagines that he possesses magical powers to melt the hearts of Democrats. Once professional Democratic campaign guys get through with him, McCain won't be melt-ing Democratic hearts—not when they find out he likes guns, opposes abortion in all ways and at all times, has an anti-union voting record, and wants to cut government spending by 10 percent.

Democrats will dislike any Republican candidate, and Re-publicans will dislike any Democratic candidate. And the number of people in the middle, who decide elections, is shrinking. According to Karl Rove, Bush's brilliant political adviser, by 2004 the size of the truly independent, truly un-aligned electorate had shrunk to 7 percent. It had been well over 20 percent throughout the 1980s and 1990s.

Now, without George W. Bush in the mix to provoke the incredibly strong emotions, both positive and negative, he evoked in the 2004 election—emotions that helped drive the highest turnout in American history, some 122 million voters, making up more than 61 percent of the electorate—perhaps the number in the middle will grow.

But in all likelihood, it won't grow much.

So if most of those with negative feelings about nominee Hillary in 2008 are already hardcore Republican voters, all her nomination will do is ensure a high Republican turnout. Of course, the kind of angry attention her nomination would receive from Republicans would allow Democrats to play jujitsu and make use of the very sorts of attacks Republicans will level against her to enrage Democrats and Democrat-leaning voters and ensure a high turnout on their end.

Thus her high negatives, in a perverse way, could inspire passionate support from Democrats who might otherwise have lukewarm feelings about her. It is certainly true among core Republican voters that few things ensure their support for a politician or a nominee for office more readily than attacks by liberals. Those attacks come in the form of major media stories that are often so grotesquely unfair they have an effect that is precisely the opposite of what is intended. Rather than driving people away from the GOP candidate, they create the sense that the GOP candidate is being unfairly trashed, give GOP campaigns a rallying cry, and help drive up turnout.

There was no need for a comparable rallying system on the liberal left until recently because the liberal Left manages the news in the United States. But the Internet has changed that, and just as Rush Limbaugh arose as a counterweight to the mainstream media, now explicitly left-wing partisan media have arisen as a counterweight to conservative media. Their purpose is to paint liberals and Democrats as victims of abuse by the mainstream media and by the "vast right-wing conspiracy" Hillary complained about in 1998.

The people who populate leftist talk radio and the leftist blogosphere are far more aware of what they hate than what they love—and what they hate are Republicans and conservatives. The hatred Republicans and conservatives feel for Hillary once endeared her to leftists. And should she become the target of right-wing scorn in the run-up to 2008, they will fall in love with her all over again. They will defend her and attack on her behalf and raise money for her and wait on lines for her and have concerts for her and do everything they did for John Kerry, a candidate no one could love.

In short, the passionate and polarized partisan populace will not consider any candidate for high office sufficiently authentic unless that candidate provokes heated opposition from the other party. It is not enough that the candidate satisfy you. Indeed, when it comes right down to it, no candidate will ever really satisfy a passionate ideologue. But it is more than sufficient if the candidate in question really, really pisses off the other team.

Thus, Hillary's high negatives may end up doing her a great deal of good. Just wait and see.

Chapter 2

AS THINGS STAND, SHE'S NOT TOO LIBERAL TO BE ELECTED

Conservatives comfort themselves with the thought that Hillary Clinton is simply too liberal to be elected president. They are actually amused by the idea that John Kerry, Northeastern liberal, might be followed as Democratic nominee by fellow Northeastern liberal Hillary. And they have some grounds for their amusement. Despite talk that Hillary has succeeded in becoming a centrist during her tenure in the Senate—talk occasioned almost exclusively by the fact that she voted for the war in Iraq and for subsequent funding measures—the American Conservative Union gave her a rating of only 9 out of a possible 100 on conservative questions in 2004.[1]

Surely, in the course of 2008, conservatives believe, the true nature of Hillary's liberalism will become clear to the American public—at which point that self-same public will turn against her. Surely given the data we've already seen, according to which twice as many Americans define themselves as conservative than as liberal, she is unelectable.

The problem with this analysis is that it smacks of a dangerous determinism that is one of the key afflictions of the contemporary Republican Party. Conservatives are so sure they hold the key to the hearts and minds of the American voter that they inevitably believe elections will go their way. Just as liberals who live in the Washington–New York–Boston–academic cocoon can't imagine that there is anyone who doesn't think George W. Bush is an idiot chimp Hitler clone, so too a great many conservatives think the electorate always agrees with them.

Conservative triumphalism has been part of Republican political orthodoxy since the election of Ronald Reagan, who added populism to the Republican mix and thereby transformed an unattractive political party into an attractive political movement. The notion of populist conservatism would once have seemed like a contradiction in terms.

Once upon a time, self-described conservatives were defined by their deep skepticism about the putative wisdom of the masses. This was due in large measure to a deeply gloomy worldview that was by turns religious, elitist, and philosophical. Religious conservatives of an earlier era believed that human beings were fallen and sinful creatures, and that their propensity toward sin made them unreliable as governors of their own hungers. Elitist conservatives believed citizens in a democracy would just be too easily swayed by the desire for goodies promised them by politicians attempting to buy their votes. In addition, democracy would inevitably lower the cultural tone of any society that adopted it fully.

Russell Kirk, author of *The Conservative Mind*, widely considered the preeminent statement of Old Right principles since its publication in 1953, said that among the "canons of conservative thought" were the "conviction that civilized society requires orders and classes [because] all . . . attempts at leveling lead to despair," that "man must put a control upon his will and his appetite, for conservatives know man to be governed more by emotion than by reason," and that "innovation is a devouring conflagration more often than it is a torch of progress."[2]

Kirk believed the only true equality was moral equality and that change was only good to the extent that it reflected the workings of Divine Providence. Profound and thought-provoking though such arguments may be, they are no basis for a political movement—and conservatism remained a haven for cranky discontents as long as Kirk-style thinking remained in the ascendancy.

That all changed with the advent of the sunny conservatism espoused by Ronald Reagan. Whether consciously or not, Reagan essentially adapted the philosophical views of Adam Smith, the prophet of the free market, to the American political marketplace. In Reagan's view, the American electorate collectively functioned as the equivalent of Smith's "invisible hand." Just as the collective buying power of the free market functions as an invisible hand guiding the marketplace, so does the American electorate as a whole, voting in presidential elections, keep the nation in balance, he believed. The failures in American politics, in Reagan's vision, derived not from voters acting foolishly but from the misbehavior of politicians. In other words, the American people know better. Always.

This notion, the idea of collective political wisdom, is profound and complex. And it is not partisan. It doesn't necessarily follow that the collective political wisdom of the American people will lead them to follow a Republican path. Alas, Republicans—like political people everywhere, who want to believe that they are the vanguard of the future—have come to equate the wisdom of the American electorate with its increased expression of support for their party. That's a dreadful mistake. Such a notion can't explain Clinton's victories, or the failure of the GOP to secure Clinton's conviction as a result of his impeachment in 1998.

When it comes to presidential elections, voters tend to choose the candidate who seems safest, who seems best suited to address the problems they are worried about. That candidate can be a political liberal. Lyndon Johnson, the paradigmatic Washington liberal president, won a landslide in 1964 in part by painting Barry Goldwater as a dangerous radical. Jimmy Carter ran as a cultural conservative against the more pragmatic, middle-of-the-road Gerry Ford in 1976. In 1992, Bill Clinton ran to George Bush the Elder's right on issues like China and tax cuts (advocating a middle-class tax cut as opposed to Bush's own 1990 tax increase). And in 1996, Clinton ran as the president who signed welfare reform and wanted to toss deadbeat dads into the pokey. In each case, these Democrats seemed the more "conservative" choice—that is, the less risky candidate, the candidate more in tune with the concerns of the electorate.

In 2008, Hillary Clinton will likewise try to position herself as the safer, better option. And some significant alterations in the American political landscape will help her make her case to the voters. First of all, despite the fact that liberalism itself isn't very popular, liberal presidential candidates have done pretty well in the past two elections. Indeed, liberal Democrats are bringing voters to the polls in far greater numbers than they ever have—far more than were ever willing to turn out for that supposed Democratic matinee idol Bill Clinton in either of his two elections.

In 2000, the combined vote total of Al Gore and Ralph Nader was 53.8 million, 3 million more than the two right-wing candidates (Bush and Buchanan) received.[3] John Kerry's 59 million votes represented an 8 percent increase over the 2000 left-liberal number. That was an astonishing achievement— just not as astonishing as Bush's 22 percent vote jump to 62 million.[4]

Can Democrats count on similar enthusiasm from their left-liberal backers come 2008? Yes. Even though they won't have the Demon Bush to kick around anymore, the fact is that left-liberals have rediscovered politics. And politics is infectious. Once you get hooked, it's hard to get it out of your blood. No matter how dispirited and disillusioned they all were from a 2000 election result they deemed illicit and a 2004 election result that broke their hearts, left-liberals will find the real prospect of backing a winner in 2008 invigorating.

They'll all be back—the MoveOn.org meet-up groupies, the nutcakes who populate the lunatic websites DailyKos.com and DemocraticUnderground.com, and the moneybags and others who poured hundreds of millions of dollars into the 2004 campaign. Let's face it: If they could raise $200 million-plus for John Kerry, a candidate so uninspiring that even his wife looked bored when he spoke, they can do it for anybody. And if billionaires George Soros and Peter Lewis don't step up to the plate this time to lead the charge by creating and funding dozens of new, independent "527" organizations—the bastard offspring of the execrable McCain-Feingold campaign-finance law, the loophole created by an effort to close loop-holes, the back door that opened when Congress and the president actually tried to close the front door to free speech—a few other guys you've never heard of certainly will.*

And what about the Republicans? Won't they be back? After all, Bush did get 62 million votes in 2004—the largest vote total in American history and the first outright major-

---

* These organizations were called "527s" after the IRS rule governing them. In the words of the invaluable OpenSecrets.org: "A tax-exempt group orga-nized under section 527 of the Internal Revenue Code to raise money for political activities including voter mobilization efforts, issue advocacy and the like. . . . Many 527s run by special interest groups raise unlimited 'soft money,' which they use for voter mobilization and certain types of issue ad-vocacy, but not for efforts that expressly advocate the election or defeat of a federal candidate or amount to electioneering communications."

ity victory in a presidential race since his father's in 1988. Add to that the success of the party in midterm elections in 2002 and maybe you're already saying, "Wait a minute. Conservative Republicans are still more likely to win than liberal Democrats."

Well, you're right and you're wrong. You're right that the perfect conservative Republican will beat any liberal Democrat. You're wrong because the perfect conservative Republican, from an electoral point of view, is retiring from the presidency in 2009.

The problem is that Bush's triumph in 2004 may be unduplicable. It was the result of very particular circumstances— a wartime president with unprecedented appeal to his party's rank and file. The leadership qualities Bush demonstrated in pursuing the War on Terror transformed him as a public figure and deepened his support with the American people (even as it spurred unprecedented anger toward him that drove Democrats to the polls as well).

But that's not the only thing that accounts for the 62 million number. For all sorts of reasons, Bush proved to have unprecedented appeal for regular Republicans and cultural conservatives. All the available data show that Bush was more popular with Republican voters in 2004 than Ronald Reagan was with Republican voters in 1984. He had support numbers in excess of 90 percent. That support allowed political genius Karl Rove and the magnificent reelection machine Rove began to design in 2001, in the wake of the unforeseen meltdown in Bush's support among conservative Christians in the last weekend of his 2000 campaign, to wring every last possible vote from red-staters.

Rove's electoral machinery used an innovative block-by-block approach to achieve unprecedented get-out-the-vote numbers. But there's only so much a block captain can do.

In the end, the candidate has to excite voters who haven't voted before or who have stayed home in previous elections, and Bush did.

So even though the machinery will still be in place to organize get-out-the-vote drives on a block-by-block level throughout the 3,309 counties of the United States, unless the candidate running for office is as attractive as Bush was, the turnout just won't be as high. This is not a problem Democrats have, because they had two pretty unattractive candidates in Al Gore and John Kerry—candidates who could not connect to voters the way Bush could—and still they did brilliantly in terms of turnout.

I KNOW WHAT you're thinking. You're thinking: Oy. Our cause is lost. Hillary wins and we lose. There's no hope.

It's not that simple. Because Republicans are, despite everything, still correct in thinking that it is harder for a liberal to win the presidency than it is for a conservative. One of the reasons that Gore and Kerry had such a difficult time breaking through and earning public admiration in 2000 and 2004 was that they were both trying to trick the American people into voting for them by pretending to be what they were not. And George W. Bush, whatever you think of him, presented himself to the American people as a person comfortable within his own skin and sure of what he believed.

The thing is, Gore and Kerry had no choice but to exude that kind of discomfort, because they *were* uncomfortable. They were hiding and they didn't know how to wear their incognito clothes. For both of them were and are liberals, quite passionate liberals (Gore a far more passionate liberal than we even knew). And they had every available piece of evidence telling them that a liberal who embraces the label and all of its baggage could not possibly become president of the United States.

What is liberalism in the twenty-first century? I suppose multivolume books could be written in an effort to answer the question, but it can be done reasonably well in a few sentences: On matters of foreign policy, liberals are all over the map, as they are on economic policy. But not on issues having to do with the way life is lived in America. On these matters, liberals are cohesive and united. Liberalism in the early twenty-first century describes a panoply of cultural attitudes toward life in America. Liberals oppose capital punishment, support gay marriage (in theory if not necessarily when it comes to liberal politicians casting votes in favor of it), believe in preferential treatment for minorities, dislike gun ownership, are uncomfortable or disgusted with the public expression of religious belief, and strongly advocate abortion on demand. These are, at best, highly controversial views that are profoundly offensive to tens of millions of Americans. If you add to that an element new to liberalism—hostility to free trade—you have a series of opinions and attitudes that the American people really don't like very much.

But what if a liberal—Hillary—could successfully hide that baggage? What if she could neutralize the liberal label more successfully than Gore and Kerry did? What if she could somehow forswear her liberalism and even claim to represent a true conservatism that has been abandoned by power-hungry and greedy Republicans? If she could do that and act comfortable with her choice and her own conduct, she might cross the Rubicon, peel off a few more voters in the middle to add to her left-liberal base, and eke out a narrow victory.

To succeed in this way, she would need the understanding and forbearance of left-liberal voters. She would need such voters, quietly and without public discussion, to accept her stealth strategy. With the subtlest of winks and nods—winks and nods so subtle that nonliberal voters wouldn't pick up on them—she would indicate to left-liberals that she is really one of them and will govern as one of them. But at the same time she would make it clear to them that if they want their share of power, they would have to allow her to say and do certain things they may detest until the November election is over.

She will need all the passion they brought to their 2004 campaign against George W. Bush even as she kind of goes against their grain and even criticizes them somewhat. It's a very tricky game. But it can be played. In fact, it was played pretty recently. And not by who you think.

See, I'll bet you thought I was going to talk about Bill Clinton and his attack on the black rapper Sister Souljah, which gave rise to the oft-used political phrase "the Sister Souljah moment"—the occasion on which someone running for office shows he's willing to be critical of elements within his own base.

In my view, Clinton has received entirely too much credit for the Sister Souljah moment, because he really didn't do anything to offend anybody with any power or cultural standing whatsoever. Sister Souljah was a not-very-popular performer who had said an unbelievably outrageous thing in the wake of the Los Angeles riots in 1992: "If black people kill black people every day," she said, "why not have a week and kill white people?" Boy, it sure took a lot of courage to criticize *that*, huh? It wasn't as if Clinton said something about an outrageous demagogue like Louis Farrakhan or Al Sharpton or even Jesse Jackson, three African-Americans whose hatemongering actually had real-world consequences. He went after a safe target with few defenders, and in the end it didn't get him much of anything. Bill Clinton was actually a centrist, not a liberal, and needed votes in the South, not in black neighborhoods.

In any case—if I may digress a little—despite the universal praise for Clinton's astounding political skills, Hillary needs to do a lot better than he did. His vote-getting record is not one any candidate seeking to win the presidency ought to be emulating. In 1992, he got only 43 percent of the vote, and in 1996 he got 49 percent, and he depended on Ross Perot stealing Republican votes in both cases to go over the top.

No, for Hillary to run as the stealth leftist, the candidacy she needs to emulate is that of George W. Bush in 2000.

Before I get going with this, you might issue a quick objection and say that Bush only prevailed in 2000 because Ralph Nader stole votes away from Gore the way Perot stole votes away from Daddy Bush in 1992 and Bob Dole in 1996. But it's far from clear that the average Nader voter would have turned out at all in 2000 if Nader himself hadn't been in the race. And Bush's own vote total in 2000 was almost surely depressed by a few million votes among his own core voters as a result of the surprise "late hit" in the last week of his campaign when it was revealed that he had been arrested for drunk driving twenty-six years earlier. The teetotaling, straitlaced segment of the cultural-conservative wing of the GOP base sat on its hands and helped account for his failure to match Gore's 51-million-vote total.

Aside from that disaster, which came as a surprise and was not the result of any specific error on Bush's part in 2000, Dubya ran a flawless campaign for president. One of the reasons it was so flawless is that, Janus-like, he showed two faces. He spent a considerable amount of time setting himself up against the prevailing orthodoxy of his own party—even as he made sure that its core voters figured out he was one of them.

It was Bush who refused to say that he was plain and simply a conservative. Rather, he was a "compassionate conservative," a message that was intended to draw a sharp distinction between him and the supposedly heartless Washington conservatives who were running Congress and whom Bush actually once accused of wanting "to balance the budget on the backs of the poor."

Bush spent much of 1999 and early 2000 stressing his differences with the conservative orthodoxy in Washington. In the fall of 1999, in a speech at the center of conservative thought in New York City, the Manhattan Institute, Bush took it upon himself to stage a direct attack on Robert Bork. Now, this was a real Sister Souljah moment, because whereas she was a nothingburger rapper, Bork was at the time as close to a sainted figure as there was in the Republican Party and the conservative movement because of the unjust treatment he received at the hands of liberal Democrats during his unsuccessful confirmation hearings for a seat on the Supreme Court in 1987.

Bork had written a book called *Slouching Towards Gomorrah*, about American cultural decline. Without mentioning him by name, Bush scolded Bork: "Too often, my party has focused on the national economy to the exclusion of all else," he said. "Too often, on social issues, my party has painted an image of America slouching toward Gomorrah."[5]

This remark sparked outrage among conservative opinion leaders, just as his statement about Republicans possibly balancing the budget on the backs of the poor did. What's interesting is that were it not for the fact that his chief contender for the Republican nomination, John McCain, seemed even more determined to offend movement conservatives, Bush might have been held to account for the hostility by Republican primary voters.

Bush found a way to neutralize the more politically noxious aspects of his coalition's philosophy by feinting a bit to the left. Hillary has already done her feint to the right with her votes in favor of the war in Iraq and defense spending. If the Democratic Party is as hungry for victory in 2008 as the GOP was in 2000, its interest groups will understand what Republican interest groups understood about Bush: She truly is one of them but needs to appear less ideologically driven than they are. Hillary gives every indication that this is the way she wants to position herself. That's what an intelligent and electable liberal must do, and Hillary Clinton is a smart and electable liberal.

Chapter 3

IF A WOMAN CAN BE ELECTED PRESIDENT— AND A WOMAN CAN— HILLARY CAN

It is perhaps the least politically correct question imaginable: Can a woman win the presidency of the United States? At first blush, the question itself seems very nearly illegal, the sort of thing that could result in the denial of tenure, or an Equal Employment Opportunity Commission investigation into views so unenlightened that they surely violate some equal-rights statute—and if not a federal violation, then perhaps a transgression of a state, city, or local human-rights ordinance. Or perhaps a conjugal punishment of a few nights on the sofa for anyone who raises it.

Lee Miringoff, who runs the Marist poll, braved the couch and asked the question in October 2005. And the results were pretty much a wash. "Twenty-six percent of registered voters say they are likely to support a woman for president regardless of whether she is a Democrat or a Republican," the poll found. "At the other extreme, 28 percent would not support a woman for the United States' top job regardless of which political party nominated her. Twenty-five percent would support a woman if she became the Democratic nominee for president, and 21 percent would support her if she were the Republican nominee."[1]

The press, as you might expect, harped on the 28 percent

who said it was not time for a female president—while ignoring the data that said 26 percent would vote for a woman regardless of party affiliation just to have a woman in the Oval Office. It was kind of a silly poll, but the data were just strong enough to suggest that any hopes of derailing Hillary strictly because of her gender are probably illusory.

Still, you can be sure that an honest public discussion of the positive and negative aspects of having a woman president will never be conducted, except in bizarre quarters among obsessives who really do believe either in male or female superiority.

There are those of the mushy-treacly feminist persuasion who would argue that a woman should be president because she will be a consensus-builder and make all the children in the United Nations play nicely together and share their oil. You'll see articles hinting at this in glossy magazines throughout 2006 and 2007. And there are those of the social–Darwinist Right who would argue that women are just not equipped by evolution to take on such a task. No glossy magazines for them. They will be consigned to websites like vdare.com that use preposterous social science to prove that the gender and race of its writers and editors are better than the genders and races of the people who don't write for them—not to mention the pages of knuckle-dragging, mouth-breathing journals like the *American Conservative.*

But while the offensive quality of the question will prevent it from being addressed in serious ways in the coming couple of years, the canny Clintons surely understand that they need to deal with it cleverly if Hillary is to win in 2008. It will not be enough for them to comfort themselves with the thought, for example, that women have won elections for positions as heads of their national governments for decades now.

It is true that Margaret Thatcher, Golda Meir, Benazir

Bhutto, Corazón Aquino, and Violeta Chamorro, among others, governed their countries. But the systems in which they were victorious were parliamentary. The women in question only had to win a local election and then prevail over other legislators to govern their own parties. Their parties, not the populace, were responsible for their becoming prime minister. As long as their parties won a plurality or majority of seats and were able in the aftermath of the election either to form a one-party government or form a coalition government with their parties in the lead, these women were the boss.

Thus, Hillary Clinton's election to the presidency would not only be a first for the United States; it would be a world-historic event. And surely there are many women—liberal women—who will be especially excited by it and would therefore do anything and everything possible to advance it. From Hillary's point of view, though, here's the rub: She will have an easier time winning the election if people don't think about her gender very much.

The liberal Left will have a choice to make. It can trumpet the sob-story aspect of a woman becoming president—how Hillary stands on the shoulders of Susan B. Anthony and Frances Perkins and Margaret Chase Smith and Gloria Steinem and Naomi Wolf and Thelma and Louise in advancing the feminist cause to the highest of heights. And it will be tempted, sorely tempted, to do so.

In an inadvertently revealing September 2005 article for *Salon*, Rebecca Traister offered an example of the sort of thing Hillary might have to contend with from people who desperately want her to win. Traister attended a party in New York to celebrate the premiere of *Commander in Chief*, the ABC series in which Geena Davis suddenly finds herself the occupant of the Oval Office. "This Tuesday," the ad line for the show ran, "a woman will become president." Marie Wilson, a feminist activist who runs an organization called the White House Project, was just beside herself with joy from the slogan alone, according to Traister: " 'Isn't that the best thing that ever happened?' asked Wilson, adding that her organization has spent years pleading with Hollywood honchos to write shows about a female president, only to be turned down. . . . Tinseltown's contribution is so vital, Wilson argued, 'because we know that you can't be what you can't see.' "

Traister then described the reaction at the party to the scene in which Geena Davis is presented to the Congress. "The moment sent chills," Traister wrote. "The audience was sniffling. Some of them perhaps hadn't been sure they'd live long enough to see this. Even on television. As the show ended, Wilson took the stage, wiping a tear from her eye. 'I must have seen this eight times,' she said, 'and I keep trying to watch it without crying.' "[2]

This sort of old-time bushwa, which treats an entire gender as though it were an oppressed minority whose every advance should be met with special tears and celebration as a triumph over adversity, is very dangerous for the Clinton campaign. You might think otherwise; you might think that you can't buy this kind of enthusiasm, or that since women make up more than 50 percent of the electorate they will be particularly moved by the first-woman message.

But you'd be wrong. The Clintons will need to quiet down the blather about the historic nature of her election and tone down the civil-rights-style "We Shall Overcome" nonsense that Marie Wilson and her ilk represent.

And this they will do. The nascent Clinton campaign will no doubt get the message out to stifle and stuff the entire discussion of Hillary's gender, because that will actually make it more possible, more likely, for her to prevail. It will surely be the case that the Left will maintain its self-discipline and wait until after her election to start shouting the feminist gospel from the rooftops. For what the Clintons understand, perhaps better than anybody else in politics, is that even though everybody blathers about the need for "change" during an election season, elections really bring out the conservative impulse in most voters.

Remember, voters usually choose the candidate who seems safest, not the one who seems more risky. Selling Hillary's candidacy as a chance to change the world would be a good way of sinking it. Voters don't want to use their vote for social engineering or as an act of symbolism. They want elections to be about *them*—about the issues they care about, the things they are concerned about. They don't want the election to be about the candidates, except to the extent that the candidates seem to be extensions of their values and core convictions.

For Hillary to win, therefore, her election has to seem like a logical extension of current political reality—the careful choice, the necessary choice. It should not seem like a hinge moment in history, an evolutionary leap. Her election has to be the more prudent option in 2008, not the more radical. If selecting her seems as portentous and meaningful as it might be billed—as the completion of a century-long process by which women have attained equal standing with men in this country—that notion will engender a quiet backlash among voters.

Ever since her emergence in 1992, liberals have been tempted to believe that Hillary is the Post-Feminist Everywoman, a reflection of the current condition of the female in America. Thus, there will be a temptation to think every American woman will see herself in Hillary and want to vote for her for that reason—or that parents of daughters would want to vote for her because her election will offer a new path for young American girls.

As Karen Burstein, a lesbian activist and longtime figure in New York Democratic politics, put it, "Hillary Clinton is the kind of person who offers little girls a model for their lives, and little boys an understanding of the promises and opportunities that exist for women. She is a woman of considerable intelligence. She's a person who has failed big and in public. And she has managed, having failed, not to be so horrified or embarrassed as to retreat into silence. Hillary has also managed to have a marriage, a child, and a career. . . . What Mrs. Clinton has vindicated over and over in her life is the notion that you do have choices, and that even if you make them and they turn out to be wrong, you can step back and go somewhere else."[3]

Well, there are plenty of women who feel just the opposite— who find Hillary a noxious example of the working woman who believes herself to be superior to the woman who puts her family and children first. And to be cold-blooded about it, if a case is made that Hillary's elevation will profoundly alter the balance between the sexes, maybe that will have a deleterious impact on her standing with male voters. Every man might see Hillary as his antithesis, and every parent might see her elevation as a thwarting of his or her *son's* ambitions.

Thus, Democrats and feminists will be doing Republicans and conservatives a favor if they carry on like the gibbering fools so many of them made of themselves when Walter Mondale named Geraldine Ferraro his vice presidential nominee in 1984. The choice of Ferraro was a stunt, nothing more, and, as it turned out, quite a bit less. It worked for a time because feminists—supposedly tough-minded, serious-thinking, worldly feminists—believed the stunt had meaning. By harping on Ferraro's gender, they made her private life—a marriage to a businessman with questionable dealings—an issue in the 1984 campaign, to Mondale's detriment. At the same time, her expectation that she would be treated with a certain degree of deference owing to her gender, and her defensiveness as well, led to her trouncing in a vice presidential debate at the hands of George H. W. Bush—whom she sternly and foolishly lectured about how offended she was by his supposedly patronizing manner.

Hillary Clinton is no Geraldine Ferraro. For one thing, she knows how to keep her temper in check in public. For another, she speaks for the most part in bromides—airless, pointless, and uncontroversial. And most important for a woman in public life, there's nothing about her private life that would surprise anybody any longer. She cannot be hurt by scandal reporting in 2008 because the damage has already been done, and she lived through it.

By far the greatest problem for Hillary, or any woman, in securing the presidency is that the qualities many people seek in the president have always been associated, fairly or unfairly, with being male.

A president is, first and foremost, a leader. And the very image that the word *leader* invokes is a masculine image, a fatherly image. Someone tough and decisive. Someone who acts, not someone who is acted upon. Whether or not these are qualities possessed by democratic leaders, whether or not these are qualities possessed by most men, their maleness is very nearly hardwired into the body politic.

This is even more true at a time when national security is a paramount concern, as it is now. The very term *national security* evokes a sense of peril from without that requires a strong protector, a guard to keep the barbarians from storming the gates. The act of providing security may require a confrontational posture, and a willingness to fight if necessary. A nation at war is a nation reliant on testosterone for its defense and for the successful resolution of its aims.

Those indefinable "leadership" qualities are the reason many Republicans quietly doubt Hillary's chances in 2008. After all, we've been a nation at war since September 2001, the ultimate challenge in leadership. And to the extent that George W. Bush has had a successful presidency, it's because people have associated him with strong leadership—by which they probably mean he is willing to use force and stick to his guns. Bush led John Kerry by nearly 20 points when pollsters asked about leadership qualities.

Bush's political problems in his second term are almost entirely due to the growing sense among the American people (including some Republicans) that his leadership isn't as strong as it was immediately after September 11. Bush doesn't need to act more like a liberal; he needs to be more of a hardass. We haven't yet prevailed in Iraq, and people are blaming Bush for that—and a case can be made that had he been tougher and more aggressive at first in the prosecution of the war against the Iraqi insurgents, we would have done better in quelling the insurgency. So the problem here is that Bush was not enough of a leader, not that (as some liberals fantasize) we should already have fled Iraq.

Bush also suffered from his reaction to Hurricane Katrina, in the immediate aftermath of which he seemed the opposite of a strong leader. He seemed remote and indecisive and not in control of his government or the situation. Basically, Bush didn't appear man enough to deal with Katrina.

Democrats believe Bush's failures in the second term are offering their best hope for change in 2008. But for them to capitalize on them and convince the American people that their candidate will be tough enough to handle the incredibly difficult problems that land on a president's desk on a daily basis, they will have to seem strong, in command, willing to make hard choices, and willing to kick ass. This is why many Republicans believe nominating a woman—nominating

Hillary—will play into the GOP's hands. If the public is looking for a tough guy, won't the public want a *guy*?

Maybe. On the other hand, if there was ever an American
woman politician who could pass for a tough guy, Hillary
Clinton is that politician. Start with the purely cosmetic.
The fact that she never quite figured out what to do with her
hair or her clothes, the fact that she's not a raving beauty,
and the fact that she has a manner that is almost pathologi-
cally unsexy all work in her favor—just as they worked
against her as a traditional First Lady. When her husband
was in office, she never tried to act demure, to recede into
the background with a faraway look, or to behave as though
her only real interest in politics resulted from her husband's
presence in it. She was a player and wanted everyone to
know it, and her attitude profoundly offended an enormous
number of Americans.

But all the qualities that made Hillary Clinton such a problematic presidential spouse may also make her just the kind
of woman people feel they can trust with the presidency.
Namely, she has created an image of herself as unfeminine,
an image that connects her to the successful female chief
executives in other countries. Golda Meir was a hard-edged
old broad, Indira Gandhi was a ballbuster, Margaret Thatcher
was a battleax. These characterizations may sound sexist.
Okay, they are sexist. But are they all that different from calling a male politician a "son of a bitch," a term many people
assign admiringly to politicians they like? Rudy Giuliani is
said to be a "son of a bitch," and that quality may have gotten
him into some hot water during his New York mayoralty—
but at the same time his often nasty demeanor gave him
some distinct negotiating advantages with his adversaries on
behalf of the causes and policies he held dear.

The same is said, in private, of George W. Bush—though
the word most commonly assigned to him is *prickly*, by

which his people mean he can sting like an immovable cactus. Or they're just adding the adverbial *-ly* to soften the word they think describes him on occasion. And certainly Bill Clinton's aides describe him as someone prone to fits of rage and chilling coldness—qualities that don't seem to match the "I Feel Your Pain" Clinton we all came to know, some of us came to love, and others of us came to be nauseated by.

The "I Feel Your Pain" stuff is of a piece with Bush's hugging and smiling and crying, which he does for conservative audiences as well as Clinton did his thing for liberal audiences. And that's the point. That stuff is almost certainly an act, a costume donned by politicians who know what qualities they lack and therefore what qualities they need to affect through force of will. So a "prickly" guy will do a lot of hugging, just as a politician with a weaker image—say, George Bush the Elder, who had to deal with a negative impression dubbed "the wimp factor"—will need to pick fights to show his strength (which is exactly what Elder Bush did by yelling at Dan Rather during a live interview in early 1988).

SO WHAT DOES all this mean for Hillary? Simple. Male pols these days have to show they have a touch of the classically feminine about them—compassion, caring, nurturing—in order (it's thought) to appeal to women. Female pols need to show they can be manly. In this way, Hillary's lack of femininity is the first, maybe the only, real political advantage her feminist toughness affords her. And it helps explain why she must be taken seriously as a powerful threat to Republicans and conservatives. She possesses a hard-to-describe style that may be the perfect blend for the first woman president.

How to describe that hard-to-describe style? It's easier at

first to describe what she is not (or what she appears not to be; for the sake of this discussion it doesn't matter in the least what she's actually like in private, as though anyone could ever get a straight answer from anybody about that one).

She is neither girlish nor womanly, neither wink-at-you cutesy nor come-over-here-and-let-me-give-you-a-hug motherly. She doesn't have a chip on her shoulder, the way Geraldine Ferraro did, but then, she is quick to assume, and almost happy to presume, that she is in the crosshairs of a massive conspiracy against her. She isn't a hair-shellacking big 'do type, like Republican Senator Kay Bailey Hutchison. Neither does she simper and flirt and act girly and sweet, like Republican senators Susan Collins and Elizabeth Dole. She doesn't rely on prettiness, like Senator Mary Landrieu. And she doesn't have the Straight-A-student demureness of Condoleezza Rice.

Hillary possesses a very complex mien. She is almost always calm and composed, but radiates an icy hauteur. When she speaks, she delivers her words in a loud monotone that has none of the breathy flirtatiousness with which so many female public figures try to seduce their audiences—and her tone ensures that the words she speaks enter and leave the ear without sticking there even for a nanosecond. She conducts herself in a fashion that seems almost to rebuff and ward off an affectionate response from someone who is watching at a distance.

These don't seem like particularly attractive qualities for a politician running in a national election. And they wouldn't be—if she were a man. A man running for president has to have at least a twinkle in his eye. He needs to give voters (and the media who follow him) a sense that there's a lot more to him than the campaign-trail automaton who delivers the same speech six times a day, seven days a week for a year—that he's not all about power and politics. He likes sports. He tells jokes. He smiles a mischievous smile. He loves his kids. Maybe he even ogles women.

It is taken for granted that a man is power-hungry and will do anything to come out on top, so he needs to have more qualities than that.

I think that for a woman to become president at this moment, she needs almost exactly the opposite. She needs to be flat. She needs to be cold. She needs to have a hard, almost unbreakable shell. She needs to seem unambiguously comfortable with wielding power, because she may have to go toe-to-toe with Kim Jong Il. She has to be a little scary, a little intimidating, a little off-putting so that she gives the impression that she can handle the crises and catastrophes that come a president's way.

That's truer now than it has ever been. Think about the demands placed on the president during the Bush years. How to respond to a terrorist attack. How to conduct a war. How to deal with a recession. How to manage a growing nuclear threat from rogue nations. How to handle a cascading series of hurricanes, one of which submerged a great American city. How to ensure that senior citizens can afford prescription drugs. Bush has to be warrior and daddy, tough guy and caring guy. There has been no letup, not a moment's respite.

For a woman to be president, she will have to demonstrate in her own person that she has transcended the qualities of traditional womanliness.

That was not an easy sentence to write, because it seems guaranteed to bring the wrath of God down on my head. The nature of the political and social discourse in America these days is designed to instill the fear of speaking honestly about such matters. It is acceptable to say that, of course, a woman can and should be president. It is not acceptable, in many quarters, to explain why voters may have an instinctive

hostile reaction to a female candidate. They will never con-
fess their not-exactly-rational feeling to pollsters, or even to
themselves unless they are ideologically antifeminist. But
people do interesting things in the privacy of the voting
booth. And if they feel that a female presidential candidate
is too much of a "woman," they will vote her down.

Should Hillary be the Democratic nominee and lose, of
course, some part of her loss will be ascribed to her gender and the fact that the American electorate is not yet
"evolved" enough. Fine. Whatever. That's the chip-on-your-
shoulder attitude Hillary must steer clear of if she is to win.
Politicians get to choose the course of their campaigns, but
they also have to play the hands they're dealt. And she will.
She will understand these naked truths, because she is a
pragmatist and because of all people in public life, she's
learned how to hear unpleasant things and come up with
strategies about how to overcome them.

———— ▬▬▬

HILLARY CLINTON LEARNED a few lessons the hard way about
referring too much to the difficulties posed by her woman-
hood. She spent much of 1992 making up for the Tammy
Wynette and "baking cookies" flubs, and never again made
the same mistakes. When she went on the attack in 1998
with her complaint against the "vast right-wing conspiracy,"
she did so without suggesting that the problem the conspiracy had with her and her husband had to do with her feminism. The self-discipline she showed in not retreating to her
place on the women's-lib barricades has served her in good
stead to this day.

The qualities that make Hillary Clinton a not especially
likable, even a dislikable, public figure are pretty good ones
for the first serious female candidate for president. For here's
the bitter truth:

The first woman president must not seem overemotional, or flighty, or guided by intuition rather than reason. She must not seem demure or delicate, nor can she seem brassy and sassy. She must not appear to be in a girlish quest of a strong man to help make things right. Above all, she must not seek to excuse any flaws in her conduct by suggesting that they are due to her being a woman—from the natural excuse, like a hormone rush jangling her emotions, to a political excuse, like an unjust society that won't give the XX chromosome an even break.

Just for vulgarity's sake, let me put it this way: She's got to be a bitch. And Hillary is a bitch. Her challenge will be to play up her antifeminine qualities without being completely without charm and appeal.

Republicans and conservatives are sure she has neither charm nor appeal. And indeed, she doesn't have much. But she probably has enough.

Chapter 4

SO SHE'S NOT WELL LIKED. SO WHAT?

Hillary just doesn't give off a pleasant or genial vibe, and that, you might think, must be a serious problem for her. After all, when Americans vote for president, they're voting for someone they're inviting into their home for four years, for someone who will peer out at them from their TV sets, give long speeches on boring topics at least twice a year that will preempt *Lost* and *My Name Is Earl,* and inevitably get into some kind of tussle with the opposing party and the press and even run afoul of a law or two. Does America want to reward itself with four or eight years of Hillary all the time?

After all, conservatives say, think back to the fall of 2004, when John Kerry was hammering George W. Bush in the presidential debates. On the one hand, Kerry clearly won those debates—or at least two of the three—because he was more fluent and less defensive than Bush. On the other hand, he was—let's not be coy here—an unbelievable drag. Whatever Bush's deficiencies as a debater, he was unquestionably easier to take than the long-winded, humorless Kerry was. It was easy to score the debates for Kerry point by point, but unless you were rooting for him beforehand, it would be hard to say that the impression Kerry made was all that favorable. And that might have made a difference in the 2004 outcome.

Hillary's likability isn't even a quality mentioned by her fans and supporters. Oh, sure, sometimes you hear that she has a loud belly laugh, or that she says colloquial things like "Okey-dokey, artichokey." She has been praised for having a good sense of humor by other senators, like Republican Lindsey Graham, who are not themselves particularly well known for having a witty side, so it's not really the most convincing testimony.

But even among those who seem to think well of her, Hillary doesn't seem to be especially well liked. Admired, perhaps; respected, evidently; a role model of a kind, to be sure. But she just doesn't ring people's chimes. So let's face it: When the nicest thing that's said about someone by her colleagues is that she's "hardworking," you're not going to win any Miss Congeniality awards. What they're really saying is that she strikes them as a kind of robot at best.

And that's really at best. Because there's just far too much information out there that suggests she really is a very difficult person, and one inclined toward unpleasantness. There is, for example, her horrendous treatment of the people she hires to write things under her own name. She insisted that the ghostwriter hired to draft her book *It Takes a Village* go entirely uncredited, and she did not acknowledge the role of Barbara Feinman Todd in any way until the matter became public knowledge. In a peculiar episode in 2005, the brilliant writer Walter Kirn published an item on Andrew Sullivan's website about a friend of his who had helped ghost Hillary's memoir, *Living History.*

"She started out all excited and impressed," Kirn wrote of Maryanne Vollers, but "I could see her spirit dimming. The problem, the woman said, was Hillary's people, who were ghostwriting the ghostwriting, angling every anecdote for effect and literally rejiggering their heroine's life. I was there in the woman's house the day the book arrived and the first thing she did with her copy was angrily hurl it against the wall. Why? Because she'd discovered that there was no Hillary, really, just a creature concocted by her people."

Vollers angrily and heatedly denied every word Kirn wrote, and he removed the item from Sullivan's blog because he didn't want to tussle with her. But how, really, could he have just made it up out of whole cloth? And for what reason? Hillary wasn't even in the news at the time he wrote it. Anyway, I believe Kirn.

If the Clinton campaign tries to convince America that Hillary is a sweet and loving and nice person who treats people impeccably and is just wonderful in every possible respect, such an effort may backfire. You can't draw blood from a stone, and you can't turn a cool customer into someone who gives you the warm-and-fuzzies. She will be sixty-one in 2008. She hasn't spent her life seducing people into liking her. She can't start now.

So the best she can be is kind of robotic. And being robotic has its virtues when you're running for president. If your goal is not to make people like you, you won't make the mistakes that politicians obsessed with popularity make. You won't try to finesse a crowd that you fear might turn on you with disastrous ad libs like John Kerry's "You know, I voted for the $87 billion before I voted against it." You will stick to your talking points and your message and never, ever deviate from them. Unlike John Kerry, Hillary is not in love with the sound of her own voice. The success she's had with silence proves she knows when to shut up. The steep learning curve of the Clinton presidency and her own run for the Senate forced her to take the measure of her own weaknesses, and she has done it with a commendable lack of vanity.

So does Hillary lose because she's not likable? Republicans would be foolish to count on it. The people who dislike her intensely now certainly won't vote for her, but as we've seen already, that huge cohort of people (40 percent) would vote against any Democrat. Which means that Hillary Hatred won't necessarily make much of a difference except for the fact that those haters will brave wind and rain and snow and sleet and locusts and frogs and the slaying of their firstborn to get to the polls on Election Day. That will help Republicans, because it practically guarantees the high turnout the GOP will need. But it doesn't make it any less possible for Hillary to make it to 50.1 percent of the vote, or 270 electoral votes, on Election Day.

Yes, Hillary is widely disliked. But for a widely disliked person, she has a surprising advantage going into the primary season. First, as we've seen, she gains from displaying her hard edge, her cold quality, to neutralize whatever negatives there might be as a result of her gender. The Democrats can take those qualities and turn them into something very positive. The word you'll hear most often from Hillary defenders and sycophants will be *steely*. That word conjures up the idea that her prickly personality and the controversies in which she has engulfed herself have somehow tempered and streamlined and forged her into something admirably tough. The steely Hillary is the Hillary who can look Iranian president Mahmoud Ahmadinejad in the eye without blinking. The steely Hillary is the Hillary who will not strike voters as a . . . well, as a woman, precisely.

Thus, Hillary won't have to try to be a bucket of charm. But she certainly will need to be a little more simpatico, just to take the edge off and give Democrats a little bit of an incentive to turn out in the same sorts of numbers for her that Republicans will turn out in to vote against her. And anybody with enough willpower can fake being a bit more simpatico, especially since the mainstream media will serve as the unofficial publicity agents for the softening of her image.

This is not something she needs to do early on in her campaign. The best role model for a quick-and-dirty image change is George W. Bush. Bush is widely considered by all except the most ornery and irrational haters to be among the more personable presidents in memory—and certainly among the most comfortable when dealing with people one-on-one. But people forget that Bush was thought to be stiff and tough and a bit edgy throughout the 2000 campaign season by everyone except those who knew him and the journalists traveling with him, who were unexpectedly amused and taken by him.

Since he didn't come across as particularly pleasant during the Republican primaries or during the long doldrums that followed until the convention, polls didn't suggest he was an especially likable character. That all changed in one fell swoop on one afternoon in an unlikely place: the West Side of Chicago, where Bush and his wife Laura journeyed to spend an hour on Oprah Winfrey's couch. Bush smiled and talked about having twins and seemed more relaxed than he had ever been in public, and with Laura by his side, the two gave off the vibe of being the anti-Clintons.

What's more, he was funny. "Where did your quick wit come from?" Oprah asked in wonder, surely having swallowed whole the Democratic caricature of Bush as a moron.

From that moment onward, Bush had Gore beat on the question of who was a more pleasant guy. An unexpected grace note like the *Oprah* appearance is really all it takes for someone's image to change—that and a demeanor during the debates that does not seem high-handed, sanctimonious, or supercilious. That sort of superior attitude is the most pronounced weakness of all major Democratic candidates, and it's what people will be looking for in Hillary as well. So long as she manages to stay on point and on target without displaying the condescending qualities that bedeviled Dukakis, Gore, and Kerry, she may effectively address her own failing in this regard. You have to figure she can make it that far. Since she doesn't possess Kerry's astounding self-regard, and she is not undone by Gore's peculiar cluelessness, she can probably pull it off.

As Rick Lazio, the Republican senatorial candidate in New York in 2000, learned to his sorrow when he faced Hillary in a one-on-one clash, her GOP rival will have to tread carefully in debate. A debate is one venue in which Hillary's gender might help her, because it may force her GOP rival to go a little easy on her—based on what happened between her and Lazio. Lazio tried to get aggressive with her at one point. He walked over to her podium, in a move that surprised her. He pulled a piece of paper out of his pocket and asked her to sign it and thereby join him in a pledge that they would both abide by campaign-finance laws.

Maybe the stunt would have worked had Lazio been debating a man. Since Lazio's rival was a woman, the moment struck far too many people as unacceptably in-her-face. The general line by the Hillary backers was that Lazio had "invaded Hillary's personal space," and by doing so, had committed some vague crime against civility or fairness. The *mot juste* to describe what Lazio had done was "unchivalrous." Voters in New York state evidently felt that even the dislikable, feminist, and unladylike Hillary deserved more genteel treatment at the hands of a younger man who was trying to play tough.

———

HILLARY CAN MAKE DO without having reservoirs of personal charm to draw from. That's what political history teaches us. Don't forget that in 2004, the anticharmer John Kerry did manage to get 59 million people to pull the lever for him. And recent political history certainly suggests that charmless politicians can have great success. Lyndon Johnson was nobody's idea of a delightful dinner partner, but he won the biggest landslide in American history in 1964. As for Richard Nixon, you probably had to be related to the guy to like him, but he managed to squeak by in one election in 1968 and win the second-biggest landslide in American history in 1972. The oleaginous promise of Jimmy Carter—"I will never lie to you"—didn't exactly suggest he was Mr. Fun Guy, but he took Gerald Ford down in 1976. George Bush the Elder spoke in an odd first-personless patter and had to tackle the general impression that he was a wimp. And though we now think of Bill Clinton as the charismatic sex god, a near-Satanic charmer, that was hardly the impression he gave off in 1992, when he ran his race with dull, emotionless precision. It was only later, when he loosened up a bit, that he became the liberal woman's Fabio. The only unalloyed charmers in the past fifty years or so were John Kennedy and Ronald Reagan, and there were plenty of people who were totally immune to their winning ways.

Hillary can be located on this continuum, and she'll have some pretty formidable help to keep her from winding up in the too-unbearable-to-be-elected column. Every joke writer in America will be desperately feeding her quips and one-liners, and somebody will make a crackerjack sentimental movie about her life that will wow the audience at the Democratic convention. Of course we conservatives and Republicans can think of nothing more unbearable, but we're never going to vote for her in any case and so we're not the audience she will be playing to.

———————

AND DON'T UNDERESTIMATE the potential appeal of her daughter, Chelsea. Having remained largely out of the spotlight for most of her life as a presidential scion, Chelsea could prove to be the secret weapon of the Hillary campaign. She is a subject of intense curiosity, and it is almost impossible even for a conservative who loathes both her parents not to feel some sympathy for what she was dragged through without her consent during the Year of Lewinsky.

Hillary may not be able to humanize herself terribly well, and the subject of her private life may tell against her. But Chelsea will have a free pass. She will be treated as sacrosanct by the media, even though she will be twenty-eight years old at the time of her mother's run. Democrats will insist on a craven double standard—it was entirely acceptable to mock and pillory the Bush twins because they had attained their majority, but better not say a thing against Chelsea or you'll be charred toast.

Imagine, for a moment, a well-crafted and touching Chelsea convention speech. That speech would not be jokey or hokey, in the manner of the joint speeches by the Bush twins or John Kerry's daughters in 2004. It would be a speech that tried to connect Hillary's own quest for power to the American dream. She can talk about what it's been like to be the daughter of a woman whose life is yet another indication of the way America can change and grow—how Hillary was able to trailblaze because the country became freer and better, and still managed to be there for Chelsea in good times and bad. And about how, as a mother, Hillary was a tiger about making sure there was a space where Chelsea could have as normal a childhood and adolescence as a life in politics and in the White House fishbowl would allow. How she would not allow Chelsea to be used as a political prop no matter how much the consultants and pollsters said it would help. How Chelsea knows better than anyone how much Hillary loves this country and how much she can contribute to its well-being, because Hillary did so much to contribute to her own well-being.

I don't know whether any of this is true or not. I only

know that little glimpses of this portrait of Chelsea's younger life have appeared in Hillary's own writings and in the statements and interviews given by Hillary apologists, and that Hillary keeps saying it because she either believes it's the truth or because it works for her. And anyway, the truth here doesn't matter, because such a speech isn't about telling a memorable story but rather about creating a feeling and leaving an impression. A serious, thoughtful, and controlled Chelsea speech would send the unmistakable message that Hillary did a good job raising a nice and poised kid under unimaginably difficult and unpleasant conditions. That is one way to soften Hillary's image without compelling Hillary to conduct herself falsely.

It may also be a way to make the subtle point that Hillary is an efficient and competent person because she did such a competent job raising Chelsea. Competence is bound to be an issue Democrats will want to harp on in 2008. They first gave competence a go in 1988, when Michael Dukakis declared that the election was "not about ideology. It is about competence." In an eerie precursor to one of the central myths of the present political moment, Democrats believed the American people agreed with them that the Reagan presidency had been disastrously managed.

George Bush the Elder and his campaign people wouldn't let Dukakis get away with it. They insisted that, yes indeedy, the election was about ideology and that Dukakis didn't want Americans to think about that because he was a Massachusetts liberal whose values were in conflict with the beliefs and wishes of the American people (oh, and by the way, they added for effect, Dukakis wasn't all that competent a governor either). And Dukakis got trounced.

———

THE CENTRAL REPUBLICAN mission against Hillary is to reignite the battle over ideology, just as it was in 1988. The fact that Democrats are so obsessed with the competence issue right now indicates that they remain nervous about advancing their own causes and convictions. That is doubly or triply true of Hillary, who needs to thread a needle in her race for the presidency. She needs liberals and leftists to believe she is on their side while reassuring moderates and those inclined to mistrust her that she isn't controlled by the ideological majordomos of the Democratic Party.

That's why competence is such an alluring campaign theme for Democrats. It's a way for them to remain closeted, to hide their true beliefs and ambitions, and instead focus the race on the Republicans and what they've done poorly. The political virtue of the competence message is that it keeps the spotlight on the GOP. It provides a way, or so Hillary and her team will think, to appeal to the hard core on the left without having to make a left-wing loyalty pledge. Hillary and her people know it is now an axiom on the left that the GOP is the greatest danger in the world—that aside from oppressing Americans at home with the Patriot Act, welfare reform, and anti–gay-marriage Constitutional amendments, abroad the GOP is a more frightening threat to world peace and stability than Osama bin Laden, the mullahs in Iran, the psycho in charge of North Korea, or just about anybody else.

But as the Dukakis example demonstrated, there's a problem with focusing on competence: It's a thin reed on which to hang a presidential bid. Hillary might be able to offer a critique of Republican incompetence, but that doesn't offer voters any guarantee that she will be more competent. And there's a logical fallacy at work: Presumably, the poor management Hillary will be criticizing will be George W. Bush's. George W. Bush won't be running for reelection, and there's only one chance in a thousand that the nominee in 2008 will be someone who worked in his administration.

At least when Dukakis went after the competence of the Reagan administration, his rival was Reagan's own vice president. Why would Virginia senator George Allen, for example, be to blame for the failings of an executive branch in which he did not serve? Why would Rudy Giuliani? If Bush is unpopular in 2008—a big if—it will be much easier to tie his successor to him on the basis of their common ideology than on competence.

Still, the competence attack is the safest route for the Democrats, and they'll take it, because they won't be able to help themselves. The greatest weakness the Democrats possess is their temptation to believe that what they read in the mainstream media about the GOP and its standing with the American people is accurate. They can't help but think the portrait of America offered by a media that is itself 90 percent Democratic is fair and accurate. That means they miss nuances. For example, everybody in the Democratic Party got very excited by a story in the *Washington Post* at the beginning of November 2005 entitled "Voter Anger Might Mean an Electoral Shift in '06." The article began, "One year before the 2006 midterm elections, Republicans are facing the most adverse political conditions of the 11 years since they vaulted to power in Congress in 1994. Powerful currents of voter unrest—including unhappiness over the war in Iraq and dissatisfaction with the leadership of President Bush—have undermined confidence in government and are stirring fears among GOP candidates of a backlash."[1]

Once again for the mainstream media, the wish that the GOP might be on track for a monumental defeat was father to the *Washington Post*'s thought. The headline and the opening paragraph—which Tod Lindberg of the *Washington Times* characterized as a front-page translation of a cheerleader squad turning itself into a human pretzel to form the phrase "Go Big D"—are not supported by the data in the article itself. As Lindberg wrote, "According to The Post's poll results, disapproval of Republicans in Congress is high, at

61 percent, but this compares to disapproval of Democrats in Congress at 54 percent. Democrats have advantages on domestic policy issues and have pulled even in handling terrorism (a serious GOP decline), but 51 percent of voters say Democrats aren't offering a clear and different direction, and 51 percent say the Republican Party has stronger leaders, compared to 35 percent for the Democrats."[2]

The mainstream-media impulse to overinterpret data boosting Democratic hopes is and will always be a secret weapon for the GOP. It provides an irresistible sense of false confidence, sealing left-of-center candidates in a happy-news bubble that impairs their ability to respond to GOP gains in areas and among constituencies toward which the mainstream media are either indifferent or downright hostile. The problem is that Washington Republicans aren't immune to the effects of the mainstream-media distortions, though they should be by now. They can overreact in their own way. They will be tempted to address the competence charge rather than ignoring it. They will be tempted to offset it by trying to change the topic to Hillary's personal shortcomings.

Operating on the assumption that Hillary's personality will be enough to defeat her is a recipe for disaster. Republicans win when they stay focused on big-picture ideas about the country, its future, and the innate wisdom of the American people. Hillary Clinton can only be defeated if Republicans convince America that her values and her ideas aren't what they want guiding the government.

Hold on, then, I can hear you saying. Hillary can't possibly win when it comes to values, considering that her husband is the man whom the lovelorn Monica Lewinsky dubbed the "Big Creep." Right?

Not necessarily.

Chapter 5

AMERICA IS TIRED OF CLINTON FATIGUE

Can the nation bear having Bill Clinton in the White House once again, even though he'll be running the East Wing rather than the West Wing? Can America stand an update and revision of that intolerable but all-consuming soap opera from the 1990s, *As the White House Turns*, only with Hillary as the occupant of the Oval Office and Bill as the neglected spouse who demands that she allow him to play a major policy role in her administration?

Back in the days when the Clinton administration was coming to a close, the answer seemed definitively to be: God, no. The nation was awash in Clinton fatigue, so much so that Al Gore spent an entire year campaigning by running the hell away from the man who made him vice president. Clinton whined about this, and his courtiers and suck-ups in the Democratic Party said that Gore was making a big mistake—but Gore was right to do it and Clinton should have had the grace to acknowledge that, during an election that was at least partially about restoring dignity to the Oval Office, he would have served his party and his potential successor better by acting as though there were no election going on around him.

It's not ludicrous for Republicans and conservatives to think that Bill may be an albatross around Hillary's neck—especially since Democrats, following in the pattern of the

2000 Clinton courtiers, are living in a state of delusion about the Clinton years and his standing with the American people.

Partisan Democrats love Bill Clinton. Actually, as Woody Allen's Alvy Singer said of Annie Hall, "*Love* is too weak a word for what I feel—I *lurve* you, you know, I *loave* you, I *luff* you, two F's, yes I have to invent, of course I—I do, don't you think I do?" This unrestrained passion for Bill Clinton is one of the odder luff matches in political history, because Clinton really didn't do Democrats very much good. His political mistakes helped lead to the Republican takeover of the Congress in 1994. He was unable to score 50 percent in his reelection bid, and in the three Congressional elections that followed the GOP takeover, Democrats were unable to take back either the House or the Senate. Worst of all, his disgraceful personal conduct in office, which led to his becoming only the second president to be impeached in American history, was the most important factor in making George W. Bush's election in 2000 possible.

And what can America make of Clinton's legacy as a leader? He will be most noted, probably, for doing things that, had a Republican done them, Democrats would have raised their voices in a cacophony of hatred. He focused his economic policy on Wall Street and the bond markets and adopted a classic Republican vision of a balanced federal budget. He signed into law the Welfare Reform Act of 1996, perhaps the most important piece of social legislation of our time but one that many liberal Democrats absolutely reviled. And he went to war unilaterally in the Balkans. Unilaterally! Without U.N. permission or say-so! (Not to mention bombing Iraq in 1998, even though U.N. Secretary-General Kofi Annan told him not to!)

So then maybe Republicans should be feeling nostalgic for the Clinton years? Well, no. Clinton may have won elections and made a difference by stealing Republican ideas, but he achieved this raging popularity among members of his own party because of his confrontations with Republicans—by waging a battle royal against the government shutdown in 1995, by turning the Whitewater investigation he himself requested into a partisan conflict with independent counsel Kenneth Starr, a conservative Republican, and by never giving an inch during the fight of his life over his affair with Monica Lewinsky and the question of whether he had bought her silence. Though ideologically anticonfrontational, Clinton gave his political all only when he was backed against a wall and was given no choice but to fight back. He never had much to show for his battle but the salvation of his own skin, but even so, nothing so rallies a party and its people as a fight to the death. He brought them to his side and told them he was fighting it for them, and when he won, it was as though they had won along with him.

And when the 1990s were over, the Republicans were still in charge on Capitol Hill and the GOP was still the party of big ideas and bold policies—but Clinton was the only one left standing from the battles of the day. So what they really love most about the guy are the battles that resulted from his own most calamitous mistakes, both politically and personally. He couldn't have won the fight over the government shutdown in 1995 if he hadn't basically handed the Congress to the GOP on a silver platter through his Hillary-inspired policy shenanigans in 1993 and 1994. And if he had kept his pants zipped and maintained just a modicum of self-control—because, after all, the American people had granted him the precious stewardship of the presidency and he owed them at least that, at least *that*—Monica Lewinsky would be a nice married lady of whom no one would ever have heard, who would be living in Westchester with a banker husband, writing checks to the Clinton for Senate campaign, and telling others in her New Mommies group about her brief time as an unpaid worker inside the White House.

There's another, far more profound and painful reason why neither Republicans nor Democrats should feel especially nostalgic for the Clinton years. It's become almost impolite to mention the elephant standing in the middle of the Clinton presidency's living room, but here goes: On Clinton's watch, he refused to take the steps necessary to snuff out Osama bin Laden and al Qaeda after they staged four major attacks on U.S. targets outside the country. He thus left al Qaeda in a position to enact the horror of 9/11.

The elephant goes unmentioned because the mainstream media have committed themselves to a ludicrous counterhistory according to which the eight months of the Bush presidency before 9/11 are more significant than the eight years of the Clinton presidency that preceded it. The Clinton elephant is there, and history will note the presence of the elephant, and history will not be kind to Bill Clinton because of it.

But forget history. What about the American electorate in 2008? What will they think of a Clinton redux? It will probably be a wash. The prospect will be pleasing to partisan Democrats, angering to partisan Republicans, and probably a matter of some indifference to the voters.

Democrats surely think Bill is an asset, and as a political strategist and fundraiser he most assuredly will be. But if they think that Bill's campaigning for Hillary and going on the stump with her will benefit her candidacy, they're nuts. Just as it will be bad for her to have too much attention placed on her gender, it will be bad if attention is paid to her marriage. She needs to run as her own person, needs even to make that point quite blatant during her run. The more time the Clintons are together, the more they are seen as a couple, the more their contiguity will serve to remind people about that achingly unpleasant time in 1998 when their marriage was an object of unholy scrutiny.

Still, the ten years' distance from that nightmare year makes it thinkable for Hillary to run a credible campaign for the presidency. The sense of embarrassment felt by many nonpartisan Americans over Bill's behavior will have faded by then. And the Bill Clinton of 2008 may not appear to be the mischief maker who held sway during his presidency. He seems to have been hit hard by the shock of discovering that he has a serious heart problem, and in the wake of his surgery he isn't acting like the rambunctious, fun-loving fellow who was circumnavigating the globe over the past few years collecting zillion-dollar speaking fees and looking like he was having the time of his life.

She acts like a different person as well—proudly trumpeting her ability to work with Republicans rather than giving close study to psychotic diagrams drawn up by lunatic pseudo-intellectual conspiracy freaks with self-important hair proving that anyone and everyone associated with the GOP is plotting against her, the way she did in the 1990s.

What's more, these days the Clintons hardly seem married. They have found a modus vivendi that has them essentially living apart, residing primarily in different houses (Hillary in Washington and Bill in Chappaqua, New York— and Little Rock, and airplanes, and wherever else he might place his pillow). This very aristocratic, nineteenth-century marital arrangement (even if it is gender-reversed) would be off-putting for any other candidate for high office, but the unusual circumstances of their relationship and the shadow it might cast over her run for office actually make it preferable to any public displays of affection or closeness between them. Her campaign would do well to highlight, however subtly, their estrangement, as it will subtly but surely help Hillary establish her own independence from her husband and offer some slight reassurance that he isn't the puppet-master controlling her from behind the marionette theater.

These are matters that the Clintons have almost certainly already taken into account. He will be all but invisible during her run—for her sake. I suppose protocol will require that he make a major speech at the convention, but that too could backfire if his address is seen as more impressive than his wife's.

So here's what I expect: I expect that Bill Clinton will speak before the Democratic National Convention, but not as himself, the former president. Rather, he will appear for seven minutes—and in that seven minutes he will *introduce Chelsea.* Following his introduction, Chelsea will speak for fifteen minutes. Bill will be center stage as Chelsea's dad, not Hillary's spouse; the proud papa, not the former president whose legacy she needs to live up to or live down, as the case may be. In other words, Bill Clinton may well represent more of a liability for Hillary than he does a practical benefit as far as playing a visible public role in the course of her campaign.

IN THIS WAY, perhaps, the Clintons can neutralize some of the inherent negatives that come along with Bill's presence. But there are other negatives that they are just going to have to soldier through—negatives that go beyond any questions raised by their marriage. For what America will be asked to do in 2008 when voting for Hillary Clinton is to participate in the creation of an entirely new kind of political dynasty. In the past, wives have followed their husbands into power, but only after the men have died, and certainly never at a presidential level.* So along with Hillary being the first female president, she would also be the first First Lady ever to emerge from the East Wing and be elected president herself (she is already the first political spouse ever to rise to high office with her more successful political husband still alive).

That's a lot of firsts, and as we've seen, Americans tend to be careful with their presidential vote and choose the less risky option. But Hillary will have the inestimable advantage of following a president who also broke through a significant dynastic barrier. Once again, her model to follow in the 2008 election won't be any Democrat, but the politician she claims to revile—George W. Bush. The current president was faced with a complex challenge during his run for the presidency. While he benefited immensely from the network of political contacts and fundraising friendships built by his father—just as Hillary will from Bill's—Bush had to appear to be entirely independent of his old man. He couldn't appear to be the second coming of a failure, which is what his father had been as a president. He both needed and wanted to chart a course entirely different from his father's in policy terms.

Bush did it by making sure his parents played almost no public role in his campaign. They did not serve as his surrogates, and only popped up every now and then to make it clear how painful it was to them to see their son being criti-

---

* In recent years, we've seen two such cases. After Congressman Sonny Bono died in a skiing accident, his widow, Mary, was appointed to fill his seat, and to the wonderment of everyone in Washington, she has remained in Congress through three subsequent elections. In a stranger case, the late Mel Carnahan actually won a Senate election in Missouri in 2000, and his abbreviated term was filled by his wife, Jean, who lost in a special election two years later.

cized. For his part, he talked about how he loved his dad and "Mother" and how important it was for him to know as a son that they loved him. No talk of tax cuts, or Saddam Hussein, or those lousy Democrats, or nothing.

Hillary's task is therefore clear. Bill might be her husband, but she needs to treat him as though he were her *father*—there to provide her with emotional support and little else. If she fails to do this, she will forever be peering out of his shadow and compared unfavorably with him when it comes to charm and political skills. And she surely knows this.

But here Hillary has a problem. Dubya really did disagree with his father's actions on the most important issues of their presidencies: how to deal with the government's role in the economy and how to conduct foreign policy. His father raised taxes; Dubya cut them. His father ran a foreign policy dedicated to world stability; Dubya's foreign policy is about changing the world for the better. So it made sense that Dubya would sideline his father. He didn't want his father's advice.

Hillary almost certainly *does* want Bill's advice. Besides which, she can't follow the turn-Bill-into-Bush-the-Elder strategy precisely, because she will want and need to use Clinton's record as president for her own purposes. That will be especially true when it comes to the economy. One of her campaign promises will be that she can return the country to the wild prosperity that reigned during the midsection of her husband's presidency, when the economic boom was so potent that it poured money into government coffers and closed the budget deficit for a couple of years. She will thereby subtly try to take credit for the lone quality of the late 1990s that everybody remembers with fond nostalgia. But she does run the risk of falling under the shadow she needs to avoid—the image that she is just running to give her husband a third term.

Fortunately, she will have the mainstream media on her side, so that won't be a problem she will have to address all that directly. And she can push it off to one side by making sure that her chief surrogate on economic matters isn't her husband, but rather Robert Rubin, Clinton's former treasury secretary and Wall Street's best-known and most-loved Democrat. The revival of Rubinomics will be the battle cry, not the revival of Clintonomics.

———————

NOW FOR THE real question this tactic raises—this and other efforts to make it appear that the new president will be more Rodham than Clinton. *How will Bill take it?* It will be a huge challenge for this monumental egotist to sit back during the campaign and play the Denis Thatcher part. He surely understands the need to do so, but can he remain disciplined? Can he restrain himself for a couple of years so that he and his wife can score the big prize they so desire in 2009?

Such restraint means no leaked stories about how he feels aggrieved he's not being paid enough heed, which is what he did to Al Gore during the 2000 campaign when Gore was keeping his distance. It means he will need to exert some party discipline to ensure that unnamed Democratic operatives, whom the media love to quote, don't go around praising him throughout 2008 in a backhanded effort to criticize her—something that won't be easy for him, because, after all, who among us doesn't love it when we hear we're better than the person who is trying to succeed us in a job, even if we are working hard to help the person get the position? Restraint of that sort requires heroism from the strongest of characters, and it will be a nearly insuperable temptation for Bill. The only thing that might keep Bill in check is his hunger for the ratification of his name and his family's place in history.

Republicans should by all means try to engage Bill and get him to fight with them on Hillary's behalf. If he succumbs to his desire to be at center stage, he will only succeed in reducing her and aggrandizing himself.

But for Republicans and conservatives who want to know how she can be stopped, let me offer you the first and perhaps the most important practical lesson of this book: Do not fight the last war. Do not bring up impeachment, or Monica, or the Starr Report, or any of it. No one needs to be reminded of it, and if you do bring it up, chances are very good the anger that will be generated by such a reminder will be directed not at Hillary, but at you.

That's what happened, of course, as the whole business was going on in the midst of the Clinton presidency. The political blame ended up being attached not to Bill or Hillary but to those who were involved in the public exposure of his personal misconduct and adultery. The same will be true in 2008. People will not want to know about it, hear about it, or be reminded of it.

But wait, some of you are surely saying. Politics ain't beanbag, and if we want to stop Hillary Clinton, we're going to have to play hardball. After all, many people thought it would be dangerous and potentially suicidal for Republicans and conservatives to revisit John Kerry's war record during 2004. And yet there's no question that the effort made by the group calling itself Swift Boat Veterans for Truth had a significant impact on the Kerry campaign. Despite being ignored by the mainstream media and shied away from by some of the more cautious conservatives, the Swiftees did the politically incorrect and controversial thing. They talked about Kerry's time in Vietnam, questioned his heroism, and called into doubt some of his grander statements about his time there. In so doing, they opened up the conversation to Kerry's extremely controversial conduct as a Vietnam veteran making false charges that American soldiers had been committing atrocities on a daily basis.

So, you say, the Swiftees drew a lot of fire, but they talked about something important and helped push Kerry's negatives way up. If the Clinton marriage will make people uncomfortable with voting for Hillary, why not go at it? The media will howl, the pundits will cry "no fair," the Hillary spin doctors will scream about the "right-wing character assassins." But hey, all's fair in love and war, no?

All's fair, maybe, but even so, you don't want to be doing things that will boomerang on you. John Kerry practically invited the Swiftees to stage their surprise attack by putting his long-ago Vietnam record at the center of his campaign. Hillary and Bill will do everything possible to keep their marriage from becoming a subject of discussion, which will mean that raising the matter will be something only their enemies do.

Besides which, the Swiftees had a story to tell that was unknown to most voters in 2004, who either had no idea what Kerry did in 1970 or weren't even alive at the time. But everyone who will cast a vote in 2008 was a sentient being when Monica's stained Gap dress and her use of Altoids as a sexual aid were front-page news. Nobody will be finding out anything new if he or she is reminded of the Clinton scandals. And if it were to come out that Bill has had a girlfriend or two since he left the presidency—which will surely be a subject of intense interest to the *National Enquirer* and the *Star*—that won't come as much of a surprise to anybody either.

In my view, the only way the Clinton sex scandal could resurface to hurt Hillary would be if the following fantasy scenario took place: Monica Lewinsky had a political awakening, got herself a subscription to the *Weekly Standard*, declared herself a neoconservative, and became a one-woman "Clinton Veteran for Truth," revealing that, say, Hillary knew all along, or Hillary sent goons to her house late at night, or something. She's the only veteran of the Clinton wars who might have an impact comparable to that of the Swiftees, and even then, maybe not. After all, the Swift Boat Veterans for Truth were themselves Vietnam War veterans and a few were bona fide American heroes. Monica Lewinsky . . . ain't.

———— ▬▬ ————

THOSE OF US who want to see Hillary stopped have to deal with the reality of the present moment. Hillary's high negatives aren't going to finish off her candidacy. Her gender isn't going to be the reason people deny her the presidency. Nor will she be denied the presidency because she isn't likable enough, or because of her train wreck of a marriage. And the fact that she is a liberal, or has done liberal things in the past, won't in itself be enough to keep her off that podium on January 20, 2009. So where does this leave those of us who want to stop Hillary? Where does it leave the Republican Party as it tries to plan for 2008?

Part II

THE 2008 LANDSCAPE: TWO PARTIES IN CRISIS

The GOP is in a difficult place. But out of that difficulty, Republicans and conservatives can find a renewed sense of purpose. And let's face it, Republicans and conservatives need a renewed sense of purpose and an infusion of energy and enthusiasm, because the struggle ahead over the next two and a half years—the struggle to defeat Hillary Clinton—is going to be rough.

Before the struggle begins in earnest, the Right needs to take a good, long, and hard look at itself in the mirror to understand where it has gone wrong and how to do a quick repair job on some of its more glaring problems to get itself in proper condition to take on Hillary and the Democrats. She and they cannot be defeated by the Republican Party in its current state. All of the GOP's weaknesses were revealed in the course of 2005—a year that Republicans hoped would be a victory lap for a party that improved its position in the House and Senate and for a president who racked up the largest vote total in American history. Instead, the GOP seemed off its game, and that gave Hillary and the Democrats the opening they needed to establish the predicates from which they will doubtless conduct the 2008 campaign: policy exhaustion, cronyism, and political corruption.

Chapter 6

THE ANNUS HORRIBILIS

The GOP got tired in 2005 for a very good reason: The last several years have been exhausting. From the moment the 2000 election refused to end, political life in the United States has been like a never-ending marathon. The thirty-six days of the Bush-Gore endgame were followed (after a month's blessed respite) by the whirlwind first eight months of the Bush presidency, which included the passage of tax cuts, education legislation, and the changeover of the executive branch from Democratic to Republican hands, department by department. Then came the unprecedented national trauma of September 11, followed a month later by the war in Afghanistan that took out the Taliban and sent al Qaeda on the run.

Ever since that victory in Afghanistan, there has been a pitched ideological battle at home. The two parties have been fighting each other over just about everything—the terms of the Patriot Act, the policy of holding stateless terrorists at our Guantánamo Bay facility, the reorganization of the government to focus on Homeland Security, the appointment of conservative judges, Social Security, how to achieve energy independence, whether to rein in trial lawyers, how to revitalize an economy in the doldrums, what to do about taxes, how to manage natural disasters both here and in Asia.

And, of course, we have fought over Iraq—whether to go

to war, how to go to war, how to fight the war, how to handle the aftermath, whether to have more troops or to bring the troops home, whether the sacrifice was worth the cost, whether the war was justified in the first place. Two hard-fought elections, in 2002 and 2004, established that the American people, though very divided, gave the advantage—however slight—on these questions to the Republican Party.

The battles have raged on since the 2004 election. Powered by anger and disappointment the way teenagers with papers due are powered by cans of Red Bull, Democrats have managed to keep themselves in fighting trim. Their negativism has been impressively relentless. Republicans, by contrast, haven't quite had the same fight in them. With Bush reelected and the GOP maintaining substantial-enough majorities in the House and Senate to make a Democratic seizure of those bodies unlikely in 2006, the GOP was left in the position of managing its gains and handling the continuation of its controversial policies.

That's not very exciting. It sure isn't as exciting as looking for any way to hand the president a defeat and do something to chip away at the GOP's hold on power, which is what Democrats did when George W. Bush asked them to help him come up with a bipartisan plan to save Social Security from a solvency crisis in the coming decade. They opposed him on what was a nice, good-government, second-term thing to do and handed him a stinging defeat.

The intensity of the opposition to Bush may have failed to derail his reelection, but its power has drained him and his small team in the second term in ways they won't admit. And it has taken its toll on the GOP as well.

The standard mainstream-media line is that the ugliness in Washington is Bush's fault. He chose to govern from the right rather than from the center and thereby alienated moderates and sympathetic Democrats. It's his bed. He should lie in it.

Now, while it is true that Bush's solution to breaking the Washington legislative logjam was to use his Republican Congressional majorities like a battering ram on major legislative issues, it's also the case that the Democrats had no interest in helping him to govern from the right or the center or the left or anywhere else. The closeness of the 2000 election and the very slim Republican margins in the House and Senate practically ensured that Democrats would wage war against Republicans in hopes of getting back into power on Capitol Hill and in the White House.

When it was in the interest of Democrats to vote with Bush—as it has been for, say, half the Democratic caucus in the Senate on high-profile matters like the Iraq War and the nomination of John Roberts as chief justice of the United States—they have done so. When it has been in their interest to trash him within an inch of his life, they've done that too.

AS I'VE SAID, Bush has been as conservative a president as the years between 2001 and 2005 would have allowed. He has governed from the right for the most part. But ask the right how doctrinaire he has been on some central questions and they'll tell you they are disappointed with some of his policy choices—in large measure because they have been very significant compromises with the Democrats and Democratic ideology.

From the time it was signed into law in early 2002, many on the right have hated the No Child Left Behind Act, a piece of legislation that was originally designed as a compendium of conservative ideas to change the hidebound public-education system in America. After the Democratic-controlled Senate got through with it, it had turned into something very different. The legislation mandates nationwide testing (something conservatives dislike but Bush likes) and increased federal spending (something conservatives despise and Democrats love). And what has Bush gotten for his compromises? Vicious attacks against the legislation from the Democrats who helped design it (like Teddy Kennedy) on the bewildering grounds that the 68 percent increase in federal education spending somehow isn't generous enough. By 2005, despite signs of modest progress in math scores, No Child Left Behind was a law with no friends.

The same is true, in spades, for the prescription-drug benefit that Bush and the Republican leadership propelled into law in the fall of 2003. Creating a new entitlement isn't anybody's idea of a conservative piece of legislation, but in this case, Bush and the GOP leadership did what they did out of stark political necessity. Had they not voted and signed that entitlement into law, the major Democratic talking point throughout 2004 would have been the failure of the Bush administration to lower the cost of prescription drugs for seniors—and it would have been an extraordinarily potent talking point. The evidence that Bush and Co. did what they had to do can be found in the Democratic response to it. Democrats opposed the Bush legislation, yet again, on the grounds that it didn't break the bank enough (because Bush sought offsetting spending cuts in some Medicare and Medicaid formulas).

So Bush boosted education spending and created a new health care entitlement (that would have been sought by any other president, Republican or Democratic). Those were bad enough, in conservative eyes. But then there was his refusal to enforce spending discipline on his fellow Republicans who run Capitol Hill. The most blatant expression, for conservatives, of runaway spending is the radical increase in the amount of Congressional pork doled out district by district. Pork is distributed by "earmarks," or mandated spending on individual projects in individual districts. The number

of earmarks rose from 4,155 in 1994 to 15,584 in 2005.[1]
Though the total cost of these earmarks is a drop in the
overall federal budget of more than $2 trillion, the outra-
geous and unseemly nature of the great majority of them
was cause enough finally to make right-wing heads explode
in 2005.

The heads exploding have belonged to two very different
types of conservatives who have come together in an unlikely alliance to express their grave dissatisfaction with the
current Washington status quo inside the Republican Party.
The first camp is made up of the old-style, green-eyeshade,
Main Street, business-of-America-is-business types whose
views dominated the presidency of George Bush the Elder.
The second comprises the more radical antigovernment libertarian Republicans, many of whom got their basic political
education from the extremely bad novels of Ayn Rand.

These two tendencies have almost nothing in common.
The old-time guys don't have a philosophical problem with
big government. They just don't like it when government
lives beyond its means. The more libertarian guys believe
government spending is an evil in itself—that it represents
the unacceptable public theft of private property and that by
fostering a reliance on government, such spending saps the
will and spirit of the people and turns them into unmanly
automata. The old-line guys think the libertarians are a
bunch of scraggly and ill-dressed zealots. The libertarians
think the old-line guys are a bunch of wimps.

What the two tendencies do have in common is a fear of
a runaway Washington, a Washington gone berserk. And
that fear seemed eminently reasonable in 1994, in light of
the Clinton health care plan, which would have effectively
nationalized one-seventh of the U.S. economy. That fear
helped ignite the Republican Revolution of 1994, when the
GOP took over both houses of Congress. Republicans then

promised to reform Washington, to clean it up, to act more responsibly.

Then, having won a gigantic mandate on that basis, Republicans discovered over the following four years that their reform agenda was a startlingly weak basis for governance. Fighting to hold the line on spending may sound like a popular thing to do—and talking about it usually is, especially when presidential candidates do it. But holding the line isn't popular in reality, because the only way to take a bite out of federal spending is to chew on programs that are overwhelmingly liked by people who vote. The Republican attempt to control Medicare costs in 1995, which was noble and necessary and tough governance of the best sort, was the cause of the government shutdown that gave Bill Clinton a new lease on life and probably led to his reelection.

The effort to eliminate Congressional earmarking—which led to a decrease in their number from that aforementioned 4,155 in 1994 to a mere 958 in 1996—proved to be a threat to the continued Republican majority in the House of Representatives. Congressmen found they didn't quite know what to tell their constituents about what they were doing to fix things and improve life in their districts. And so the reformers decided basically that they were going to say, "What the hell, we're not going to reform ourselves out of a job." In time for the 1998 elections, earmarks were back up to 2,100, with every congressman and senator getting his or her taste, Democrats as well as Republicans. The economic boom was pouring so much money into governmental coffers that they could spend at will on these little bitty programs and still claim to have helped balance the budget. Republicans learned to stop worrying and love the pork.

Even though earmarks were growing in number, the Republican Congress continued to do what it had been elected to do—it kept a check on Democratic spending ambitions. The dynamic between the Democratic president and the Republican Congress throughout the 1990s created a budgetary standoff when it came to big-ticket items. There is an advantage to divided government: It means that neither party can simply exert its will.

That advantage disappeared in 2001, when George W. Bush came to power. Republicans found themselves simultaneously in charge of the executive and legislative branches for the first time since 1953. With the exception of the seventeen months when the Senate fell into Democratic hands because a lone liberal Republican defected in mid-2001, the GOP has maintained its control.

Both the White House and the Congress have determined that the best way to hold on to power is to work together as much as possible. The House and Senate have largely done what Bush wanted them to do. And Bush has shown his gratitude by not turning against his own party and its wants and needs on Capitol Hill. The idea that some conservatives have had, which is that Bush needs to go and kick Congress in the pants for its big-spending ways, has a touching naïveté about it.

The simple fact of the matter is that Bush can't go on the offensive against the priorities of Republican senators and representatives. To do so means that he will lose their acquiescence and support on the things he wants and needs that they don't care much about. Somebody once did come to Washington and make war on his own party's Congressional leadership in the name of good government. That somebody's name was Jimmy Carter, who was not only the worst president of the modern era but also, by leaps and bounds, the least effective and the most bumbling.

Besides, Bush and the current Republican leadership in Congress are neither libertarians nor green-eyeshade Main Street types. They have basically bought into the central argument of supply-side economics, which is that what matters is large-scale economic growth created by cutting taxes and allowing private markets to do what they do best with the money of individual taxpayers. For supply-siders, big-government spending is probably not a great idea, but it's not a problem in and of itself if the economy is booming— because if the economy grows, tax revenues to the government grow even after taxes are cut. Once again, that idea proved itself correct when the economic boom of 2004–2005 brought in so much new money to the government that the budget deficit opened up by the recession of 2001 shrank by 20 percent in a single year.

———————

TRUTH TO TELL, had things gone swimmingly for Bush and the GOP in 2005, the attack on him and Congressional Republicans for their free-spending ways probably wouldn't have gained much traction. But by the late summer of 2005, the forced march of Bush-era politics began to take its toll on a somewhat punchy administration that had already done more and taken on more in four years than most two-term presidencies have had to contend with. The management got sloppy, and the administration became defensive about its sloppiness and retreated into insularity when what it needed was fresh air streaming in from the outside.

The news from Iraq has seesawed between amazing progress on the political front to a fairly continuous stream of sad news about American casualties. The economy has shown itself to be extremely strong, but the combination of world demand and natural disaster conspired to raise gas and oil prices to painful levels and thereby obscure the good economic news. And a once-adept and responsive White House was suddenly incapable of doing anything right.

In August 2005, when antiwar activists and their friends in the mainstream media decided to make a living martyr out of the politically daft mother of a tragically killed American soldier who set up a PR machine disguised as an itinerant camp near Bush's home in Texas, the administration's lack of energy became especially pronounced. Conservatives on blogs, in magazines, and in newspapers went to the mattresses to defend the war and its purpose against the Cindy Sheehan machine. But the White House, fearful of looking as though it was either beating up on a mourning mother or not wanting to elevate her criticisms, did little or nothing.

That was followed by the politically disastrous stutter-step response to the flooding of New Orleans and the Gulf Coast by Hurricane Katrina—when Bush's tone-deafness in the first seventy-two hours allowed hysteria to take over the media and Democrats eager to use the disaster as Exhibit A in their case that Bush either didn't care about people or couldn't do anything right or had a government run by cronies or wanted to kill black people or was hoping to cancel Christmas. As details emerged in subsequent weeks and months, it would become clear that the grossest failings were those of the mayor of New Orleans and the governor of Louisiana, two Democrats who were only too happy to fob off the blame for their astonishing misconduct on the Bush administration. In the end, the 7,900 people who were plucked from the rooftops and flooded buildings and the hundreds of thousands who became refugees inside the United States were all saved by the federal government—which acted quickly enough to stem the waters, plug the levees, and ensure that the projected death toll of 10,000 or more would actually end up being a tenth of that unimaginable number.

The image of Republican incompetence painted by the media in the wake of Katrina was a case of misdirected projection. The Katrina hysteria wasn't really about New Orleans. It was, rather, about Iraq. The mindset was this: It was no wonder the Bushites couldn't handle Katrina, since they had mishandled Iraq so badly. The self-congratulatory line about the media coverage of the devastation of New Orleans—coverage

that, subsequent events proved without doubt, was uninformed, slanderous, wrongheaded, and unfair—was that the
disaster had finally awakened the press from its supposed
slumber about the evils of the Bush administration. This was
a bizarre line of praise and attack, since the coverage of the
Bush efforts in Iraq had been almost uniformly negative from
about three minutes after the statue of Saddam was toppled in
that Baghdad square.

Indeed, the coverage of Iraq has played right into the terrorist insurgency's strategy to dispirit Americans and Iraqis
and to embolden enemies of the United States. Because the
insurgents were proving so fiendishly difficult to crush, the
more sober and serious opposition to the Bush administration's strategy in Iraq decided this state of affairs provided
retroactive proof that Bush had bungled the war in the first
place and shouldn't have attempted it at all. At the same
time, the unserious but more politically potent opposition
continued to argue that Bush had "lied" us into war by pre-
senting universally accepted evidence of Saddam's weapons
of mass destruction. Taken together, the serious and unserious opposition cases had tilted the country against the war,
at least as far as polls suggested.

The national distress about the (falsely) perceived lack of
progress in Iraq was the trigger for the barbaric yawp about
Katrina. Conservative pundits joined in, at least to some degree. On the *National Review* website only minutes after
Bush delivered his first speech on Katrina relief efforts, I
wrote, "What a lousy speech . . . Everybody on the Right better wise up and fast. Bush blew this first one big time, and
needs to be prodded to improve, not apologized for. Don't defend him just because you know liberals are going to attack,
and don't come up with bizarro theories about how he's a
man of action not reflection etc. etc. He emoted plenty
around 9/11. Look, it's not too much to say that the contin-

ued viability of his presidency resides in how he and the administration respond in the next week."

I was not alone. Hard-charging columnist-blogger Michelle Malkin spoke for many conservatives when she scoffed at President Bush for having praised Michael Brown, director of the Federal Emergency Management Agency. Brown had been outrageously unprepared for this disaster, but Bush had told him, "Brownie, you're doing a heck of a job." Malkin wrote, "Really? 'Brownie's' job is to direct the federal response to natural disasters such as Hurricane Katrina. . . . This is not the time to give a weak performer the benefit of the doubt. The FEMA director's role in the ongoing recovery effort is too important to be entrusted to a clueless political hack with such poor judgment. Rather than praise Michael Brown, Bush should fire him." Bush did fire Brown a few days later, and the conservatives calmed down a bit.

And so a nation reeling from two massive hurricanes and high gas prices and a really crummy second-season opener of *Desperate Housewives* limped into October. Whereupon it suddenly occurred to everybody that the special prosecutor looking into the leak of a CIA operative's name in 2003 was going to be finishing up his work by the end of the month. Considering the year Bush had been having, there was every reason to believe the special-prosecutor news was going to be calamitous for him. The rumors all over Washington suggested a neutron bomb was about to hit his administration, with as many as twenty-two senior officials indicted for participating in a conspiracy in the leaking of CIA operative Valerie Plame's name—including Karl Rove, the president's closest political adviser and his friend of thirty years' standing.

The anxiety was fostered and fed by the potent Democratic Left, which was desperate to believe that special prosecutor Patrick Fitzgerald might do for them in the courthouse what they could not do at the ballot box—neutralize and perhaps destroy George W. Bush and all he stands for. They convinced themselves that the alleged crime Fitzgerald was investigating might even have been worse than Watergate. The day of the indictments, they told each other on their outrageous and outrageously popular websites, would be as thrilling as December 25. They dubbed it "Fitzmas."

Sorry, T. S. Eliot, but April 2005 was positively balmy compared with October, the cruelest month Republicans had suffered since Bill Clinton's impeachment trial ended in ignominy in 1999. For during that very same period, House Majority Leader Tom DeLay found himself indicted as well, but not by a straight-arrow guy like Fitzgerald. DeLay had the misfortune and the great luck of being Javerted by a transparently partisan prosecutor in Texas whose infamous gall was only exceeded by his comic bumbling. That prosecutor, Ronnie Earle, charged DeLay with a crime he could not have committed—because the law with which DeLay was charged had not been passed at the time he was alleged to have behaved illegally—and used as evidence for that crime a single document that he then lost. No matter. The Earle indictment meant that the extremely effective DeLay—perhaps the most technically skilled legislative leader of our time—had to resign his leadership post from the House of Representatives. Which was Earle's real goal. His original charge was later dismissed by a judge, but by this point Earle had secured two other indictments that allowed the case against DeLay to go forward.

At the same time, the Senate majority leader found himself in some trouble as well. The very, very rich Bill Frist sold off his stake in his brother's mammoth hospital business a month before the stock tanked. Supposedly, that stock had been held in a blind trust, but then documents turned up suggesting Frist had seen records of all the activities in his trust—which by definition meant it would not have exactly been blind.

There was some good news in October, but it just didn't penetrate. In an election that saw a turnout rate of 61 percent, nearly four-fifths of those Iraqis who voted ratified the country's new draft constitution. And here at home, the economy surprised everyone when news came that it grew at the sizzling rate of 3.8 percent in the third quarter of 2005, even as the states of Louisiana and Mississippi effectively stopped having an economy at all. "The U.S. economy appears to retain important forward momentum," said the outgoing chairman of the Federal Reserve Board, Alan Greenspan— mild-sounding words that, for the opaque Greenspan, were the equivalent of jumping up and down and shouting hooray. Because of the increased economic activity, the federal budget deficit for 2005 was 20 percent lower than anyone had predicted.

Even Fitzmas turned out to be a bit of a bust, as special prosecutor Fitzgerald indicted only one senior White House official. The indictments themselves were relatively petty at that. Fitzgerald specifically said he was not alleging that there had been any sort of White House conspiracy in the Plame leak. Relieved Republicans joked that the Dems all got coal in their stockings on Fitzmas.

Still, the overwhelming anxiety got to Republicans. Some of them began to act as though they were thinking about dumping their Bush stock and selling at a loss. Out of nowhere, right-wing websites began debating whether Bush was or was not a "true conservative," and the expressions of passionate discontent were far more aggressive than the efforts to defend Bush against the charge.

What really set off the Autumn of Our Discontent was the single most boneheaded act of the presidency—Bush's decision to pick his Texas buddy, lawyer, and loyal staffer Harriet

Miers to fill the Supreme Court seat left vacant by the retirement of Sandra Day O'Connor. At the age of sixty-one, with more than thirty years' experience as a lawyer, Miers was a nonentity to all but Bush himself—a person so unimpressive that White House staffers who had been in dozens of meetings with her during the Bush years couldn't remember her ever saying a single word.

It was a galling selection that struck at the heart of the conservative movement—but not for the simplistic reasons given by the mainstream media, which understand the Right about as well as I can follow a game of cricket. Rather, for the first time in his presidency, Bush had decided to be cavalier about one of the two or three issues that conservatives take the most seriously.

IT'S WORTH DWELLING on this matter for a while, because it offers a way into understanding the direction we Republicans and conservatives must take to find our way out of the doldrums. It means understanding the way in which the conservative movement has found unity in surprising ways and on the most important matters facing the country—and how that unity has helped move the Republican Party to act both wisely and shrewdly time and again. It means understanding that if Republicans and conservatives fight on a matter of conviction, they can win against GOP go-along-to-get-along-ism.

The rise of the Right these past forty years has largely been made possible by a surprising congruence between two divergent strains in the American body politic. On the one hand, there's the populist strain, which expresses itself in the form of grassroots organizing to effect political change from the ground up. On the other hand, there's the elitist strain, which expresses itself in the promulgation and dis-

cussion of ideas about how the world should work and how
to get there.

You would think that elitists and populists would have a
hard time working together, but on the right these past
decades, they've blended pretty well. And nowhere has the
blend been more effective than in relation to the judiciary—
or, more precisely, when it comes to the matter of how the
American judiciary should conduct itself.

This third coequal branch of government has been the subject of an extraordinarily serious examination by the elites on
the right over the past forty years. In fact, the intellectual
backlash against the effort by unelected liberal judges with
lifetime tenure to write law from the bench rather than leaving that task to the duly elected representatives of the people
was a key impetus in the creation of a modern conservative
intelligentsia. Nonleftist intellectuals saw in the activist liberal judiciary an implicit threat to the Constitutional balance
set out in 1789—a threat to democracy itself, since the cardi-
nal principle of democracy is that the people make the laws
rather than an unelected elite.

And so the work began—in the writings of Robert Bork,
among others. Those writings hit many young law students
with the force of revelation. They decided to join the intellectual battle for the soul of the judiciary—writing law review
articles, securing clerkships, even creating an organization
called the Federalist Society that was dedicated to the propo-
sition that judges needed to interpret the Constitution as it
was written and not use it as a tool to work their will with no
check on their power. (Rarely if ever has there been an intellectual movement as oddly modest as the Federalist movement. Intellectuals almost never want to circumscribe the
authority of the field to which they have devoted their life's
work—to limit its power.)

The intellectuals have managed to make common cause

with grassroots activists who don't have the time or inclina-
tion for the abstract theoretical points of legal theory. The
Right's grassroots activists are enraged by the behavior of
the judiciary not because they worry about the Constitutional balance of powers or legal niceties but because they
don't like what the judiciary has done. They don't like abortion on demand. They don't like racial preferences. They
don't like judges who seem to sympathize more with the
woes of criminals than they seem to care about the mon-
strosities criminals inflict on ordinary people.

Both the populists and the elitists of the conservative judicial coalition recognize that there's no appealing the Supreme
Court, that the only way to push back against the liberal judicial assault is to ensure that the right judges are chosen. That
means electing the right politicians. Thus the two groups
work together, with the grassroots activists giving force to
the intellectuals' efforts to change the judiciary, and the intellectuals advancing the grassroots activists' cause in the
most high-toned and cerebral manner possible. By 2005, this
conservative judicial coalition was poised for triumph.

When the Supreme Court's swing justice, Sandra Day
O'Connor, retired that summer, President Bush chose as her
replacement the elegant, calm, poised, and eminently serious John Roberts. After an initial hesitation, both the grass-
rootsniks and the intellectuals were very pleased with the
president's selection.

The grace and ease with which Roberts handled himself
testified to the sophistication of the conservative judicial
cause. And the sharp, literate wit he demonstrated in memo-
randa he wrote during his years in the Reagan administration—
as when he quipped about an award program for women who
change professions after the age of thirty that "some might
question whether encouraging homemakers to become lawyers contributes to the common good, but I suppose that is for

the judges to decide"—indicated that he would bring a formidable, skeptical, and unconventional intelligence to his job.
Conservatives were therefore delighted when, after the death
of William Rehnquist, President Bush chose Roberts to be the
new chief justice.

The Roberts pick validated the conservative approach to
the judiciary, because a judge who was so clearly aligned
with the modest approach had proved himself so spectacu-
larly qualified for the position that even twenty-two grudg-
ing Democrats in the Senate voted to confirm him. And
that's why the president's selection of Harriet Miers to fill
the O'Connor seat felt like a vicious slap in the face. For
while Bush clearly thought Miers would satisfy those who
sought a conservative judiciary, he was instead treating
these steadfast supporters of his administration with deep, if
unknowing, disrespect.

Miers had never been a part of the conservative efforts to
fight the liberal judiciary. That much was clear from the fact
that nobody but Bush and some people in Texas knew who
she was or where she stood on any matter. Her lack of a public record on hot-button issues was alluring to the president,
because she might be able to appear uncontroversial and
therefore go through without much of a tussle—particularly
since the Democratic leader in the Senate, Harry Reid, had
suggested Miers might be a good choice.

Bush and his team let the Right know, through leaks and
private conversations, that Miers was an evangelical Christian and therefore pro-life. She would be a reliable vote to
overturn *Roe v. Wade* should that opportunity ever arise.
That, Bush thought, would suffice. What he failed to understand was how insulting that line of thought was to the intellectual wing of the conservative judicial movement—the
suggestion that Miers should be trusted to be a good justice
because her own personal beliefs on abortion would have led

her to do what conservative intellectuals wanted in relation to *Roe v. Wade*. And her selection was an insult not just to the intellectuals but to many of the activists as well, who had spent enough time with the intellectuals to understand how important the role of ideas has been in the effort to stop the runaway judiciary.

The conservative intellectual argument against *Roe v. Wade* hasn't been about abortion at all. Since the decision was handed down in 1973, conservative thinkers have been arguing against *Roe v. Wade* as a matter of constitutional law, on the grounds that it represented an unconscionable intrusion of the judiciary into the lawmaking role of the legislative branch. Now, abortion backers have consistently poohpoohed that notion. They claim that the intellectual case against *Roe* is merely a convenience—that conservatives just want to get rid of abortion, and will use any argument to get there.

Abortion backers fail to understand the difference between the intellectuals and the activists. Unquestionably, the primary goal of the activist wing of the conservative judicial movement has been to overturn *Roe* because of a profound opposition to abortion on demand. But that hasn't been the dominating approach when it comes to judicial selection in any of the three Republican administrations that followed the *Roe* decision.

In the '80s, Democrats constantly attacked the Reagan and Bush administrations for supposedly imposing an abortion "litmus test" on judicial nominees. The attackers got it wrong. Yes indeed, there was a Reagan and Bush-the-Elder litmus test of sorts when it came to picking judges. Yes, it involved abortion. But it wasn't about abortion—it was about the *Roe* decision. The issue for Reaganites who vetted potential judicial nominees was not whether abortion on demand ought to be legal. (Some actually thought it should be.) The issue was the Supreme Court's finding that abortion was a right guaranteed by the Constitution.

Since Justice Harry Blackmun, who wrote the majority opinion in *Roe*, could find no language in the Constitution relating to abortion or any procedure remotely similar to it, he instead located the constitutional right to abortion in the "penumbras" of the document. Under such vague terms, almost anything could be called a constitutional right as long as five justices wanted to declare it so. Blackmun's ruling, to the eyes of conservative legal intellectuals, cut the courts free of any mooring in the Constitution. Even worse was the judiciary's theft of lawmaking power from the elected representatives who are charged by the Constitution with making new law.

Should abortion be legal? Nothing in the Constitution said it could not be legal.* Even as *Roe* was being heard, many states were changing their laws—including California, where the not-yet-pro-life Ronald Reagan signed abortion legislation into law. Congress could have taken it up as well, and had there been a major national debate about the matter that would have been settled through the actions of the elected representatives of the people, it is fair to say that one major battlefield in the American culture war might never have been opened.

The Reagan-era litmus test was not, "Are you pro-life?" Rather, it was, "Do you have an original understanding of the Constitution?" Which meant, roughly, "Do you believe the Constitution is a document that means what it says, or

---

* It is true that many in the pro-life movement think abortion should be considered a violation of the Fourteenth Amendment rights of the unborn, on the grounds that the unborn are being denied equal protection. But in the real world of politics, that argument is so far away from consideration that it can barely be considered in the present context.

do you believe its meaning changes over time depending on what judges want it to say?" There was no interest in how a person's faith might play a role when it came to the issue of abortion. The judicial selectors in the 1980s wanted to know whether that potential judge was going to "legislate from the bench," which was unacceptable, or would "strictly interpret the Constitution," which was the only acceptable answer.

With the Miers nomination, Bush reversed all that. Gone was the intellectual case against judicial activism. Instead, he was asking the Right, implicitly, to support Miers because her heart was supposedly in the right place, not because her mind was. Bush was basically demanding that conservative intellectuals support a choice he had made on a fundamentally anti-intellectual basis. That was bad enough. Worse, everything that became known about Miers in the course of her twenty-four days of fame in October 2005 tended to suggest that Bush might well have pegged her wrong. While she might have voted to overturn *Roe* for whatever reason she might possess, she did not have similar leanings in a conservative antiactivist direction when it came to issues like affirmative action—issues at least as important to the intellectual wing as abortion was.

What happened as a result of the Miers nomination was something without precedent. For while the leading grassroots activists in the conservative judicial alliance had expressed their support for Miers because of the assurances about her pro-life views, the intellectuals went ballistic. These were some of the most durable and steadfast supporters of the Bush administration, and they (we) felt deserted at a critical moment when they (we) were among the only voices expressing support for it and for him. It was their (our) relentless critiques of the nomination, Miers's questionable fitness for one of the most powerful positions in the

United States, the faulty reasoning in the few public arguments she had made, and the unlikelihood that she would prevail in grueling Senate hearings that helped scuttle her nomination.

Calm was immediately restored on the right three days after Fitzmas failed to bring down the administration, when Bush turned around and nominated the distinguished jurist Samuel Alito to the O'Connor seat. Alito was, like Roberts, very nearly the Platonic example of what a modern conservative jurist could and should be. Peace broke out on the right.

The fight over Miers was vital because at a moment of political depression and ideological disappointment, the coalition between the populists and the intellectuals on the right came together to fight a good fight—to make a stand on principle. In so doing, they helped lead the Bush administration out of the doldrums at exactly the moment it needed to emerge from them. These are the people—the people who generate and popularize ideas and the activists who spread those ideas outward to the grassroots—who will be crucial to any effort to defeat Hillary.

———

THE ANNUS HORRIBILIS, however, exposed certain fault lines and structural weaknesses within the GOP that need to be addressed if the party is to move forward in the coming two elections.

Chapter 7

THE GRASSROOTS GROWL AND THE SIREN SONG OF SCHISM

Political movements must take the long view if they are to succeed. Movements aim to change the entire context of the national discussion, and that can't be done in a month or a year. The status quo is always jealous of its prerogatives and resists efforts to retire it, often with barrels blazing. At any given moment during a time of change, the forces of change will usually be under attack. They will be accused of arrogance, foolishness, fecklessness, cruelty, shortsightedness, criminality, and venality. Their opponents will attack them for taking needless risks with the lives of their fellow citizens, for their arrogance in the assertion that things must change, and for incompetence in executing change.

But while political movements need to take the long view, political parties in the United States don't have that luxury. Their candidates for national elective office face the voters every two years. And despite the fact that members of the House of Representatives have a 95 percent reelection rate and sitting senators are only rarely kicked out of office, American politicians maintain a surprisingly healthy fear of the electorate and its wrath. If the voting public is giving off an unhappy vibe, politicians get uneasy—and if things don't seem to be changing for the better very quickly, they often panic.

The condition of the Republican Party in the first decade

of the new millennium is a case in point. The GOP's control in Washington was solidified and deepened because of a change agent named George W. Bush, whose willingness to risk the wrath of the status quo in pursuit of change succeeded beyond anybody's expectation. He took the reins despite an incredibly weak hold on the presidency after the disputed election of 2000, and in two succeeding elections his policies were instrumental in securing and strengthening the GOP's hold on the House and Senate.

But, said Bush's fellow elected Republicans as his second term began to founder in the fifth year of his presidency, *that was yesterday. What have you done for me today?* Washington's elected Republicans know that Bush never again has to face the voters, because he is term-limited. They do, and with their life raft threatening to sink, they gave off every indication that it was every-man-for-himself time. Senate Republicans supported a resolution on Iraq calling on the president to give quarterly reports to them demonstrating that he was trying to scurry out of Iraq. The Senate also voted 90–9 on an amendment to ban torture, even though torture is already illegal under U.S. law—a piece of legislation designed by Republican John McCain that could only be seen as a slap at the administration. A lone Republican senator, Olympia Snowe of Maine, successfully kept an extension of Bush's capital-gains tax cut from being considered in 2005.

The division between elected Republicans in Washington and the Republican president who kept them in power was yet another depressing indication of just how easy it is for the GOP to come apart whenever it faces difficulty, especially when it comes to the Senate. (Because there are four times as many House members as there are senators, the individual conduct or vote of a member of Congress tends to be far less meaningful—and the way the rules are structured in the House makes party apostasy seem far less attractive than in the Senate.)

The temptation to go your own way is especially great for a Republican politician, because he is usually rewarded for it. For two decades, conservatives have ruefully noted how any public figure on the right who comes out against conservative orthodoxy in favor of liberal orthodoxy is bathed in an intoxicating and addictive shower of approval. The Right refers to this phenomenon, with thick irony, as "growing"—shorthand for "growing in office," which is how liberal editorialists described the ideological journeys of Reagan appointees who once seemed hard-line, like Surgeon General C. Everett Koop and especially Supreme Court justice Anthony Kennedy. To go from scorned to beloved is a heady experience for anyone, and for public figures it's clearly an endorphin rush more powerful than crack.

The most ludicrous recent example is the most pointedly and aggressively anti-Bush politician in the Republican Party, Nebraska senator Chuck Hagel. Hagel has spent the Bush years finding fault with very nearly every Bush policy under the sun—which is par for the course for Hagel, who clearly confuses his own wisdom on all matters worldly with that of his homophone, the German philosopher.

This rather extreme maverick is almost entirely without friends in the GOP and the source of immense irritation among conservative activists. And yet whenever stories are done on possible Republican presidential candidates, Chuck Hagel's name is invariably mentioned. The thing is, given how profoundly he has alienated vast swaths of his party, Hagel is about as likely a future resident of 1600 Pennsylvania Avenue as I am.

But it's not just mavericks in love with the sound of their own voices who are tempted by the siren song of schism. A quick look into the 2008 crystal ball suggests that almost every major Republican politician likely to make a run for the presidential nomination is threatened by the possibility of a split in the GOP ranks. The threat doesn't come from elected politicians this time, but rather from the party's ideological and organizational base—its grassroots activists and the leaders of influential groups. The ideological gatekeepers in the Republican coalition are going to make it tough on everyone who runs. If their displeasure is incurred, there's no telling what they might do. They don't mind hinting that they will pick up their marbles and go home if the party nominates a candidate that doesn't say everything they want to hear.

Sometimes those tempted toward schism are more Machiavelli than Hegel/Hagel—more interested in being feared than in being loved, because they don't expect to get the love and therefore are more than willing to settle for scaring people into doing things their way. The problem is that there are many ideological gatekeepers and their demands are, at times, contradictory.

The potential schismatics were out in force in 2005, firing warning shots across the bows of Republican politicians with the clear implication that their dissatisfaction might take a more forceful and dangerous turn in 2008. For example, the issue that has come to occupy more passionate and heated attention from potential schismatics than any other is illegal immigration. Immigration has become a meta-issue on the right, a melting pot in which a dozen other concerns have been tossed.

There's the issue of American national self-identity—how the immigration from Mexico threatens that because Mexicans seem far less interested in becoming American and more interested in remaining Mexican in America. There's the issue of government-provided benefits—how citizens are now paying for social services for non-Americans who are themselves required to do nothing but be on American soil to receive them. And there is the issue of national security—whether the porous borders offer an unparalleled opportunity to terrorists.

These are all powerful concerns and vitally important issues. They must be addressed. But the discussion of illegal immigration has gone far beyond a policy dispute into another realm entirely—a realm of passion. Those who believe the porousness of our borders is a crisis above all others can barely keep their temper with anyone who does not share this view. The anti-immigration activists believe their single issue is so important it will dwarf all others in the years to come, and that tens of millions of Americans are so worked up by the monstrousness of illegal immigration that they will rise against it.

"This is the one issue from which all others flow," according to Jim Gilchrist, who was one of the founders of a vigilante border-patrol group called the Minutemen. "It's the one issue that puts our future prosperity and security into jeopardy."[1]

Gilchrist and other anti-immigration voices had a devil of a time containing their anger at George W. Bush, who possesses a more expansive and optimistic view of the matter. They reviled Bush's proposal to convert illegal immigrants into "guest workers" who are required to return home after a three-year stint in the United States. Indeed, when he first issued it in late 2003, the reaction from the conservative grass roots was so vociferously negative that he tabled it for two years.

There's one problem with the idea that illegal immigration is the paramount issue today: it has yet to be borne out in any way by electoral results. There were two test cases in 2005. In Virginia, GOP candidate Jerry Kilgore became convinced illegal immigration was a winning issue when he attended meetings with voters and found voluble citizens pounding on the tables about it. He sought to use it in debate against Democratic rival Tim Kaine, and ran a much-discussed commercial about it: "What part of 'illegal' does Tim Kaine not understand?" Of course, Kilgore lost. Immigration did nothing to lift his prospects, and some think it might have hurt him a bit in Northern Virginia's very ethnically diverse suburbs.

The second test came later in the year, when Gilchrist himself was one of the candidates in a special-election runoff for a Congressional seat in California. His showing in the initial race was extremely unimpressive. He received only 14 percent of the vote, but because the Republican candidate didn't get 50 percent, Gilchrist lived to keep running on his single issue. He increased his share of the vote in the special election to 25 percent, but with lower turnout than in the first balloting a month earlier. "The hard truth," wrote the California-based blogger Hugh Hewitt, is that "there is a small, but important anti-illegal-immigrant vote. [But] it is less than 10 percent in one of the most conservative Congressional districts in the country. . . . Despite massive media attention and around-the-clock boosterism from local radio flacks, the candidacy of anti-illegal-immigration single issue candidate Jim Gilchrist could only muster . . . less than one third of the [losing Democratic] vote in November of 2004. No 'Minuteman' candidate will ever have more favorable conditions than this special election, and still the Minuteman candidate failed miserably."[2]

The problem with provocative issues that cause voices to grow very loud and insistent when they are discussed is that it becomes all too easy for politicians like Kilgore to overestimate their appeal. It's also hard for those who are advocates on a given matter to have an objective sense of their issue's reach, because it's all they talk about and they can sometimes forget that what they talk about isn't what other people talk about. Gilchrist and the anti-immigration foes became convinced that he did brilliantly because he received a mere 23,000 votes.

But for true believers, it doesn't necessarily matter how popular an issue is with voters. If they are interested in changing the direction of politics, they don't measure their effectiveness by elections alone. Single-issue obsessives know there's one quick and dirty way to get as much attention as possible for their cause, especially in Republican politics. And that's to create a presidential candidacy based on it. In 1996, the idealistic and wealthy magazine publisher Steve Forbes chose that route because he wanted to create momentum and buzz for a flat tax. And he succeeded, to some extent, beyond his wildest dreams. He actually won the Republican primaries in Arizona and Delaware. And by entering the primaries in 2000, he forced George W. Bush to advance an aggressive tax-cut proposal to prevent Forbes from outflanking him in the New Hampshire primary.

It's almost certainly the case that someone will run in the 2008 Republican primaries as the anti-immigration candidate. That someone will probably be Tom Tancredo, a Colorado congressman who has become the loudest anti-immigration voice in Washington. The question is whether people like Gilchrist will accept the inevitable defeat of the Tancredo candidacy—and the almost-certain refusal of the victorious candidate to take a very hard line on immigration.

For whoever does win the Republican nomination in 2008 will be faced with an unacceptable risk of offending Hispanic voters if he adopts an anti-immigration position—the Hispanic voters whose willingness to vote for George W. Bush in decent numbers was a key contributor to his 2000 and 2004 victories. And there will be no assurance that an anti-immigration stand can replace the voters he will almost certainly lose for doing so. That refusal to adopt the anti-immigration line will anger the Tancredo-ites, and in their anger they will hear the siren song of schism singing to them. They will be tempted to follow in the footsteps of Patrick J. Buchanan, the columnist who ran a protest candidacy against George Bush the Elder in the primaries in 1992, ran to lesser effect in 1996, left the GOP in 1999, and ran two campaigns for president in 2000 and 2004 whose clear purpose was to sink the Republican nominee.*

If the race for president in 2008 is very close and an anti-immigration party can score a million votes, that won't make the case that there is a groundswell of American sentiment against illegal immigration (since 1 million votes out of 122 million amounts to a measly 0.8 percent). But if 20,000 or 30,000 of those votes come in certain close states, they could swing the election.

And the question the immigration schismatics will have to ask themselves is whether they want to bear the responsibility for having contributed to the election of Hillary Rodham Clinton. Will the Republican candidate for president, whatever his name, be so deserving of punishment for his heterodoxy that Hillary's ascension to the White House would be preferable?

That's what's wrong with the politics-as-punishment strategy: The punisher ends up becoming the punished.

———————

THE DESIRE TO ENFORCE political discipline through punitive measures has become an unfortunate aspect of contemporary politics on the right. We saw it in action when Senate Republicans joined seven centrist Democrats in May 2005 in an alliance that preserved the Senate's right to filibuster in

———————

* Instead, in the greatest political irony of modern times, his presence on the ballot in Florida's Palm Beach County inadvertently helped give George W. Bush the presidency. God has a sense of humor.

exchange for ending filibusters against several Bush judicial nominees. Many conservatives reacted with fury to the deal. The man some consider the most powerful activist in the Religious Right is James Dobson, who runs the immensely influential Focus on the Family. Dobson, like many others, was hopeful that Republican politicians would take the opportunity of Democrats stalemating conservative judges to invoke the "nuclear option"—a change in Senate rules that would mark an end to the unprecedented use of the filibuster against appeals-court and circuit-court judicial nominees.

"This one hit me personally harder than I think anything ever has coming out of Washington," Dobson said. Now, that was an astonishing statement. Could it be that the tirelessly pro-life Dobson was more upset by the filibuster deal than he was, say, by the 1992 Supreme Court ruling that upheld *Roe v. Wade*? Wasn't the character assassination and subsequent rejection of Robert Bork's nomination to the Supreme Court more upsetting? I could name about fifty things that probably bothered him more. How could a compromise between senators having to do with a relatively arcane procedural loophole be a catastrophe for the ages?

Since it was almost certainly impossible that a political deal like the one on judges could have hit Dobson harder than either of those, one has to assume that his violent reaction was, in part, a conscious and deliberate choice—a Grassroots Growl. "This Senate agreement," he boomed, "represents a complete bailout and betrayal by a cabal of Republicans and a great victory for united Democrats."[3]

While Dobson growled, the Family Research Council—a grassroots organization Dobson founded but which since has gone its own way—acted. One of the seven Republicans who signed the deal was Mike DeWine of Ohio. The Family Research Council targeted him. Eight days after the deal was struck, the council ran radio commercials attacking DeWine in Ohio. This was very nearly unprecedented. DeWine was

not up for reelection in 2005, and in any case it was un-
heard-of for a Republican-aligned organization to run attack
ads against a GOP politician whose record was otherwise
perfectly acceptable. He received a 100 percent conservative
rating on social issues from the *National Journal* and is a
stalwart pro-lifer. But that just made it even worse for Dobson and the Family Research Council. They expected such
behavior from John McCain, who was thought to be the or-
ganizer of the filibuster deal—and as for the five liberal Republican types who joined McCain, what could you do with
them but shake your head?

But Mike DeWine? He was one of their own. When Dobson used the word *betrayal*, it was DeWine more than anyone he must have been referring to. There could be nothing
worse than a traitor, and that is what DeWine seemed to him.

While Mike DeWine may not have been seeking office in
2005, his son Pat was. The younger DeWine was a candidate
in a special election for a Congressional seat, and he got
pummeled in the primary.*

The reason Dobson and Co. were so adamant about the
need to end the filibuster was to ensure that Democrats
could not use the tactic against a conservative Supreme
Court nominee, the most important issue for the social
Right. Which made it all the more astounding that Dobson
threw his support behind George Bush's ill-considered and
ill-fated nomination of Harriet Miers to the court almost
instantly—pretty much solely on the basis of a phone call
from Karl Rove assuring him that Miers was opposed to
abortion. After all, at least DeWine's decision to back the filibuster deal did lead to the approval of seven conservative

---

* He lost to a bonehead named Jean Schmidt, who made herself infamous
only a few months into her term by suggesting that Congressman John
Murtha—a war hero with his own boneheaded ideas about pulling out of
Iraq—was a coward. There isn't much to celebrate about Schmidt's victory.

Bush judges. If Miers had made it to the court in part due to
Dobson's support, she might well have gone another way—
the way of Souter.

Just as the filibuster fight was really about the Supreme
Court, so too the DeWine fight was really about the direction
of the GOP in the upcoming election. Dobson and the Family
Research Council wanted to put a major fright into the party's
politicians, to let the word go forth that whatever your prior
record, if you are judged wanting in any way, you will not
only be opposed but publicly attacked. The Family Research
Council's Grassroots Growl at DeWine was the logical next
step after another GOP-aligned group, the Club for Growth,
took the inventive tack of supporting primary challengers to
sitting elected Republicans through the use of aggressive
media campaigns. In 2000, the Club ran commercials against
liberal Republican representative Marge Roukema. Two years
later, its chief target was Wayne Gilchrest, a liberal Republican congressman from Maryland. And in 2004, it sought the
defeat of Republican senator Arlen Specter by the far more
conservative Pat Toomey.

In none of these cases did the Club for Growth's Grassroots
Growl succeed in ousting these incumbents, but it did put the
fear of Growl into Republican Washington. "I always say politicians are cowards," the club's founder, Stephen Moore, once
put it, "and they really are. We say we're going to run someone against them, and they start wetting their pants."[4]

The Club for Growth was itself following in the footsteps of
Grover Norquist, the Republican activist who, in 1986, came
up with the simple but brilliant notion of asking politicians to
put their signature where their mouth was on the issue of
taxes. He asked all officeholders and seekers to sign a "pledge"
guaranteeing that they would "oppose and vote against any
and all efforts to increase taxes." The flip side of the pledge, of
course, was that anyone caught violating it would be shark
bait for an opponent who could quote the pledge's words

against its faithless taker—as happened, most notably, to George Bush the Elder when he discovered just how fatal it was to his political career to break the "no new taxes" promise he had made during his presidential bid in 1988.

Of course, the pledge approach doesn't take into account what happens if the pledge is broken and the candidate who breaks it loses. He won't necessarily be replaced by someone pleasing to those who were angered by the violation of the pledge. Indeed, it's far more likely that his successor will be much worse. In 1993, Bill Clinton became president in part because of Bush the Elder's violation of his promise—and then Clinton turned around and signed tax increases of $33 billion, far larger than the ones Bush had agreed to in 1990.

It's a mark of the conservative coalition's commitment to ideas that its activists are so interested in a politician's stated convictions. But there is another, less attractive aspect of the Grassroots Growl. Sometimes it is issued not because the grassroots groups are standing on principle but because they are asserting their dominance and want politicians to submit to them. Or because they just want a little stroking. Stroking is what Dobson got from Karl Rove when Rove called him on the morning of the Miers nomination. It's hard not to think that Dobson was so pleased to have been paid obeisance in this manner that he let that override his common sense.*

---

* Here's what Dobson said about the matter on the radio: "Karl Rove had shared with me her judicial philosophy, which was consistent with the promises that President Bush had made when he was campaigning. . . . Mr. Rove assured me in that telephone conversation that Harriet Miers fit that description and that the president knew her well enough to say so with complete confidence. . . . I would not say much about the phone call from Karl Rove, even though I'm very close to many of the people who are on the telephone. Why would I not do that? Because it was a confidential conversation and I've had a long-standing policy of not going out and revealing things that are said to me in confidence. That may come from my training as a psychologist, where you hear all sorts of things that you can't go out and talk about."

Look, if those are the rules of the game these days, then that's how politicians will have to play to get elected and get the presidential nomination. This is the great, possibly politically fatal, failing of John McCain, the Republican senator from Arizona and former GOP presidential hopeful who runs first or second in every poll of putative 2008 candidates. In many respects, McCain should be an ideal candidate for the Religious Right. He has an unimpeachable pro-life voting record. He is highly critical of the No Child Left Behind Act, the Bush education bill that religious conservatives abhor. He is a strong advocate for Second Amendment rights. He has a record on defense issues second to none. And for nearly twenty-five years in the House and Senate, he has been one of the most ardent budget-cutters and big-government opponents in Washington.

And yet most leaders of the Religious Right would tell you, point-blank, that McCain would be an entirely unacceptable presidential candidate for the GOP—that they would work day and night to keep it from happening and they would view his candidacy as a dagger aimed at the heart of their movement.

In part, their disaffection is the result of profound policy differences. On economic matters, McCain does not support growth-oriented economics. He voted against the Bush tax cuts twice and drove a huge cigarette-tax increase through the Congress. And his signature piece of legislation, the McCain-Feingold campaign-finance bill, was explicitly designed to limit the power of grassroots activists by making it harder for them to raise money—and most appalling for anyone who treasures political speech, by banning television and radio advertising by such groups in the sixty days preceding an election (thirty days preceding a primary). Since advertising is one of the key ways grassroots groups exert their influence on the political process, one can see why a politician who tries to stifle them would be on their enemies list.

But their distaste for McCain goes even deeper than that. In 2000, when McCain was running for president, most of the Religious Right had already lined up with George W. Bush (with the notable exception of Gary Bauer, who ran for president himself that year as the faith-based candidate and threw his support to McCain)—in part because of the campaign-finance views McCain had expressed.

McCain grew so angered by the tactics used by some grassroots groups, especially in a hard-fought primary in South Carolina, that he gave an uncommonly vituperative speech in which he implicitly likened the Religious Right to the moneylenders working inside the Temple: "Those who purport to be defenders of our party, but who in reality have lost confidence in the Republican message, are attacking me, they are people who have turned good causes into businesses. . . . I am a pro-life, pro-family, fiscal conservative, and advocate of a strong defense. And yet, Pat Robertson, Jerry Falwell and a few Washington leaders of the pro-life movement call me an unacceptable presidential candidate. They distort my pro-life positions and smear the reputations of my supporters. Why? Because I don't pander to them, because I don't ascribe to their failed philosophy that money is our message. . . . Just as we embrace working people, we embrace the fine members of the religious conservative community. But that does not mean that we will pander to their self-appointed leaders. . . . Apparently, appeals to patriotism can only be heard by card-carrying Republicans, and only certain Republicans at that."[5]

McCain was careful to say that Dobson, among others, was "changing America for the better." But there was no blunting the message. McCain wagered that there were more Republican voters disgusted with the Religious Right than there were Religious Right voters, even though every piece of data should have told him the opposite. By speaking so aggressively, and by asserting that the personal attacks on his candidacy were nothing less than threats to the Republican Party and the United States, McCain turned himself from an opponent of the Religious Right into its enemy. Given that the 22 percent increase in Republican turnout in 2004 came in part from Karl Rove's mining of Christian support—and given that Republicans are going to need a comparably enthusiastic turnout from those voters in 2008 to defeat Hillary—McCain's 2000 wager has to be counted as one of the dumbest political acts in recent history.

Is this a fence he can mend? It's very, very doubtful. And because of that, it's highly unlikely that McCain could win his party's nomination in 2008 despite his poll standings.

IT'S IMPORTANT TO TRY a thought experiment about what might happen if McCain were somehow to emerge from a difficult primary battle as the likely Republican nominee for the presidency—important because it raises the basic question any Republican disappointed in his possible choices for 2008 will have to answer.

During the primaries themselves, the schismatics would insist that they could never support McCain were he to become the GOP nominee. Angry conservatives on talk radio and on blogs would bitterly note how McCain's passionate following in the media makes him inherently untrustworthy. From Dobson and the Family Research Council and others there would be quiet, cold, angry talk about the need for a third-party candidacy. Indeed, the name that would be floated most frequently as the third-party candidate in this talk would be Dobson's, on the grounds that he has a radio audience 7 million strong and a grassroots organization second to none.

President George W. Bush, on his way out of office, would be under immense pressure from party regulars to try to heal the division between McCain and the schismatics. And he would almost surely try to do so. But could a lame-duck president really heal these deep wounds? And given McCain's flinty and combative character, would he be willing to do what was necessary to please the schismatics—like, say, agreeing to push a social-conservative attack on gay marriage that might get Tim Russert, Chris Matthews, and the media McCainiacs all hot and bothered?

This would be the political news story to end all political news stories, especially in the spring of 2008, after Hillary Clinton secures the Democratic nomination. In the slow season between the primaries and the conventions, the media need something a little more spicy than "there's a race coming up." And what could be spicier than a potential Republican Party crack-up? Dobson would instantly become the most famous man in America—especially because the mainstream media would like nothing more than to send the GOP into oblivion, all the while smiling innocently because, hey, this is a fight between Republicans and you can't call us biased in favor of liberals just because we're giving wall-to-wall, twenty-four-hour, gleeful coverage of the destruction of the party we all hate.

At times like these, even a Dobson—even a sworn enemy of the mainstream media—can become a Hagel, a Republican who becomes a media favorite because he bashes other Republicans. Dobson is not a publicity hound, to put it mildly, but there's no question that newsmagazine covers and new photos of you posted every seventeen minutes on the Drudge Report can fulfill one of man's most basic hungers.

Maybe the breach can be healed. Maybe Dobson—or whoever—can be wooed and won and convinced to rejoin the GOP team. But even so, immense damage will have been done to any effort to stop Hillary Clinton from becoming president. In a situation where there is Republican-on-Republican bloodletting well into the late spring and summer of 2008, Hillary may not have to do anything but stand there and play it safe until November to take it all.

This little guessing game suggests two things: First, McCain might want to think long and hard about whether running for president is a good idea for him, his party, or his country.* Second, conservatives need to be very careful over the next two years. With a candidate as formidable as Hillary, who as president will be in a position to do serious damage to the causes grassroots activists hold dear and to the country as a whole, schism simply isn't an option. Whatever emotional satisfactions schism can provide are not worth the immense cost of indulging them.

It's said that on July 4, 1776, the day America was born, John Hancock affixed his signature to the Declaration of Independence and reminded the assembled Congress, "We must all hang together." To which the legendary wag Benjamin Franklin is reputed to have responded, "We must, indeed, all hang together, or most assuredly we shall all hang separately."

Republicans and conservatives need to keep those words in mind come 2008.

---

* And yes, I say this as someone who supported McCain in the Republican primaries in 2000.

Chapter 8

THE NOT-REPUBLICAN PARTY AND THE NEO-LOONY LEFT

Hillary Clinton and the Democrats are hoping that the political debate in the United States over the next two years will concentrate exclusively on the sins, perceived and actual, of Republicans. And who could blame them? If Republican shortcomings are the sole subject of the national discourse on politics and leadership, then Democrats will get a free pass in the 2006 and 2008 elections—unless there is a drastic and complete turnaround in the negative public attitudes toward Republican politicians, in which case the referendum on Republican rule will benefit the GOP and harm the Democrats.

Such a turnaround seems unlikely. There are just too many actual and potential sources of trouble. There's the traditional weakening of a president's party during his second term—though if the Reagan and Clinton presidencies are any guide, as the president's term actually reaches its last few months, it's met by a wave of prenostalgic good feeling. That wave helped George Bush the Elder secure a landslide victory in 1988, but it didn't do anything to improve Republican prospects in the House or the Senate, where the GOP lost ground in 1986 and 1988. And unless there is a radical improvement in the security situation inside Iraq, Republicans and Bush will continue to suffer from the public frustration over the war.

Even if a Republican turnaround doesn't occur, however, Democrats will face a problem of their own. While it's certainly true that their relentless attacks on the GOP have taken their toll on Bush and the Republicans, and that the good news on the economy and on Iraq didn't seem to affect a grumpy body politic (according to one October 2005 poll, 68 percent of respondents said the country was on the "wrong track"[1]), the trouble for the Democrats is that their attacks haven't helped their own case much, if at all. Consider: In the fall of 2005, the discussion in Washington centered on polling data that showed a meltdown in support for Bush and the GOP. Over the course of that year, the president's approval rating descended from 52 percent to 37 percent in the Gallup poll, while the overall approval rating of Republicans in Congress dropped 9 points. But the approval rating of Democrats in Congress *also* fell by 9 points.[2] In fact, at least one poll—Harris Interactive—showed that the public had a less favorable view of Democratic senators and congressmen (25 percent) than of Republicans (27 percent).[3]

After most elections, both parties have had enough of fussing and fighting and need some downtime. But after losing the 2004 election, Democrats decided they didn't have the luxury of slacking off, and they made a conscious decision to go on the offensive against Bush and the Republicans. Their first major move was to select Howard Dean as the chairman of the Democratic National Committee—Howard Dean, among whose public statements when he was running for the job was "I hate the Republicans and everything they stand for." That's 37 percent of the electorate Dean was talking about. That's 43 million people. That's a whole lot of people for the chairman of one of the two major political parties in the United States to hate.

The bitter loss of the 2004 election had the effect of pushing the party to the left, at least rhetorically. It was clear from the near victory that the Democratic Party had been re-vivified by money and passion pouring in from its unapolo-getic left flank—which, according to Byron York's seminal reporting, raised more than $200 million independently of the party apparatus and in total outraised and outspent Re-publicans for the first time in a quarter-century.[4] Kerry lost, but the passion remained, and as the second Bush term pro-gressed, an astonishing number of mainstream Democrats blended in with the party's leftist flank, following the Democratic leaders in the House of Representatives and the U.S. Senate. The central plank of the second-term anti-Republican platform was what the Left's had been ever since the middle of 2003: that George W. Bush deliberately lied when he said Iraq had weapons of mass destruction.

This notion was and is demented on its face: If Bush knew Iraq was free of WMD, why would he have made such a case out of it when the world would discover the truth once the war was over? Or if he was such a Machiavellian master-mind that he determined to go to war for no reason and in-vented one he knew to be nonexistent, why didn't Bush have his trusted military aides plant some WMD somewhere?

So much for the logic of the "Bush lied" meme. But forget logic and think about the politics of the argument. At first blush, continuing and deepening this line of attack didn't seem to make a whole lot of sense. Why, in 2005, should the political discussion in the United States remain fixated on what happened in 2002 and 2003? After all, an entire elec-tion had already pivoted on the issue of Iraq, and for the first time in four elections the American people had returned a clear majority vote for George W. Bush, who staked his re-election on staying the course in Iraq. Voters are, we've al-ways been told, interested in the future, not the past.

That may be true of voters, but that doesn't mean it's true about those Americans who don't vote. The 2005 polls were not polls of voters, and that fact made them qualitatively different from the polls in the two preceding years. In the run-ups to elections, polling firms use screening techniques to make sure they include among their sample only Americans who say they will actually cast a ballot. Those screens are expensive and time-consuming, and as we've all learned, of questionable accuracy. Once an election is over, however, most firms drop their registered-voter or likely-voter screens and instead include all Americans in their sample. This saves them money and makes their job a lot easier. But it means that the polls don't necessarily track with the data pollsters collected during the preceding two years.*

Something else happens when you don't screen for voters. Simply put, you widen the pool so much that it includes entirely uninformed Americans—the kinds of people who couldn't name their own senator and probably have no idea who else is in the government besides Bush and Cheney. This matters, because those who don't actually follow the news are still vaguely aware of what's going on through the penumbras and emanations of the popular culture. It is precisely such people who can be reached by the simple vulgarity of the "Bush lied" message. To believe it, you either have to be extremely sophisticated—the sophistication of the sort that can write an alternative history of the past four years that omits every single piece of information that exculpates Bush from the "liar" charge—or pretty ignorant. There's not much middle ground there.

Having hit on a message that had some appeal to the apa-

---

* It does, however, mean that it is fair to compare such polls with others taken in the same way during other presidencies—say, Reagan in 1985 and Clinton in 1997. And such comparisons are not favorable to Bush, whose mid-30s numbers contrasted painfully to Reagan's 60 percent and Clinton's 55 percent.

thetic American who only knows about politicians because of what he sees in the movies, Democrats lucked out further. Bush and the Republicans chose to ignore their attacks and act as though the criticism didn't matter. They were determined to change the subject after the election to domestic matters—to Social Security reform and a new energy policy. Bush would not argue with Democrats over Iraq. And that turned out to be a huge mistake, because Bush let his adversaries dominate the discussion for most of the year, and they dominated it by harping on the same talking point endlessly.

Incessant repetition has its political virtues. Indeed, all successful political messages are implanted through the use of obsessive repetition, especially when there are media outlets eager and willing to hear the message and amplify it. The yelling and shouting and screaming by the country's leading Democrats—by the House and Senate minority leaders, by Howard Dean, and by Democratic presidential candidates John Kerry and Al Gore—created an echo-chamber effect that reverberated outward through the mainstream media. And once Vice President Dick Cheney's chief of staff, Scooter Libby, was indicted for lying to a grand jury, the "Bush lied" message finally got purchase. By the late fall of 2005, the polls demonstrated, the American public was saying it no longer found the president trustworthy—and the Republican Party was cratering.

But here's the thing: The Democrats hurt themselves as well. As noted, the ugliness of the political discourse in 2005 drove their poll numbers down just as much as the Republican numbers dropped. And while Democrats were thrilled at the thought that a Rasmussen Reports poll at the end of the year asking which party the public preferred in upcoming elections featured a 9-point advantage for Democrats, they conveniently forgot that the same poll taken just before the

2004 election showed a 6-point advantage for Democrats—and their party still lost seats.

The public just did not seem comfortable with the Democratic approach on political matters. In a November poll taken by the *Cook Political Report*, 52 percent of respondents said that when Democrats criticized Bush on the subject of Iraq, they were doing so to "gain a partisan political advantage" (only 30 percent said the criticisms were an effort to help win the war). More damaging still, 70 percent of people said that criticism of the war by Democratic senators hurt troop morale. Even 55 percent of those who called themselves Democrats said criticism was damaging to morale. Only 21 percent of them said it helped morale.[5]

What docs this all mean? You could look at it the way Tod Lindberg did and quip cleverly, "All this proves is that if a party wants to commit suicide by doing everything to drive the other party's numbers down, it can do so at will." So the Democrats' assault on Bush's Iraq policy might have been a victory only in the sense that the Greek general Pyrrhus understood it. According to Plutarch, after Pyrrhus's troops finally prevailed in a ruinous battle with the Romans, the general "replied to a friend who celebrated his victory that one more like it would utterly undo him."

But I don't think the attack on Republican honesty was a Pyrrhic victory for Democrats. It was wrong, unfair, and profoundly dishonest. Strictly as a matter of pure electoral political strategy, though, Democrats had no other choice but to go for Bush's jugular. Had Democrats gone easier on Bush and sought accommodation with the president, they would have added a cherry on the top of his sweet 2004 victory. The nation might have been happier with all its politicians for getting along and playing nicely together, and would doubtless have felt more positive about the war in Iraq. But playing nice would not have helped the Democratic Party's cause in any way. Quite the opposite. In an era of good feeling, the party in power gets the credit even if the party out of power doesn't get much in the way of blame. A civil 2005 would only have increased the possibility of more Republican pick-ups in the House and Senate come 2006 and the increasing marginalization of the Democratic Party in Washington.

And Democrats had reason to be terrified. The hidden story of the Bush years has not just been the president's ability to harness the power of the presidency, but the entirely unexpected surge of Republican strength down-ticket as well. In 2002, Republicans led by Bush returned the Senate to GOP control with a stunning 5-seat pickup, and then increased their strength in 2004. They are going into the 2006 elections with a nearly insuperable 10-seat Senate advantage.

The story is similar in the House of Representatives—an 8-seat pickup in 2002, followed by a 3-seat pickup in 2004. Some of that increased strength was due to the change in the Congressional map following the 2000 census, which took seats away from Democratic states and gave them to solidly Republican states—as well as maneuvering in Texas to ensure a more favorable electoral outcome for the GOP in the House. Despite the close division of the vote at the presidential level in both 2000 and 2004, it appeared that Republicans could have been on the verge of establishing a hold on Congress that might rival the uninterrupted forty-year run of the Democrats in holding on to the House before 1994.

The Democrats could not just lie down and die. And they didn't.

———

THOUGH THE PUBLIC says it loves consensus and abhors petty fighting, the nation's two-party system demands a Hegelian dialectic. If Bush says "yes," then unless there is extremely good reason to do otherwise, Democrats are compelled by the very nature of political discourse to say "no" right back. That's what they did when Bush said there was a Social Security crisis and then demanded that Congress devise a plan for him to sign that took care of it. Democrats took the politically wise, if generationally irresponsible, step of just saying no. They took the same tack when it came to his energy policy and the idea of making some of his tax cuts permanent. Bush says yes, they say no.

But Democrats did cross the line in 2005: They engaged in an effort to delegitimize a war in full swing that involved 159,000 U.S. troops—troops whose cause and sacrifice were being belittled and downgraded by a national debate suggesting their deployment to Iraq was the product of a Republican lie. By banging on the same discredited drum in 2005 that they had banged on from the summer of 2003 through the election of 2004, by claiming that the Republican president had knowingly led the country to war for an indiscernible reason, they chose to use the tragedies of war as a fundraising, organizing, and conspiracy-mongering tool. Effective it may have been, but it was cheap and low.

And it was so wildly irresponsible—even in the eyes of the Democrats doing it—that after months of making the argument that Iraq was basically a lost cause and celebrating war-hero-hawk Congressman John Murtha's proposal for an "immediate redeployment" of American troops from Iraq, Democrats could not actually bring themselves to make an official case for a pullout. The day after Murtha emerged with his proposal, Republicans brought a modified version of it up for a vote on the floor of the House. Democrats reacted with outrage at this supposed "stunt" that was, pure and simple, a matter of calling their bluff. Bluff called, they folded. Only three Democrats out of 202 voted for an immediate withdrawal.

You could almost argue that the 403–3 vote against the Murtha proposal was a moment of clarity in American politics. When push came to shove, elected officials who had been deliberately trying to delegitimize the war effort came to their senses after months of ugliness and did something responsible for a change.

You could, however, also offer a different argument—a far darker argument, and one that has the delicious ironic advantage of feeding from the same conspiracy trough at which the porcine Democrats had been stuffing themselves all year. To wit, Democrats refused to vote to pull American troops out immediately because, despite their antiwar message, they had developed a perverse interest in seeing the war continue to slog along just as it had been.

After all, opposing the Bush administration's actions in Iraq had bound the Democratic Party together from the summer of 2003 onward and had been its key organizing and fundraising tool. All the passion in the party had been directed toward the idea that the war in Iraq has been nothing but a ruinous calamity for America and the world. Hundreds of millions of dollars was raised in 2004 to effect the goal of removing George W. Bush from power because he invaded Iraq. That money, in turn, helped generate an enormous grassroots effort that brought an unprecedented 59 million people to the polls to vote for a Democrat. And it wasn't Bush's tax cuts, or his No Child Left Behind Act, or his interest in establishing a free-trade zone with South America that got them there. It wasn't his desire to drill for oil in Africa that got them there either. It was Iraq.

Whether Democrats voted for the war (as John Kerry did) or against it (as, say, Howard Dean would have had he been in the Senate), they all came together with an overriding interest in punishing George W. Bush for having made the decision to invade—either because the decision was wrong to begin with or because his supposed mishandling of the situation inside Iraq after the fall of Saddam Hussein proved he was an incompetent clown. He had to go. He was, as many and maybe most Democrats came to believe, "the worst president ever."

So Bush's war in Iraq brought Democrats together as never before, and expanded the party's vote by 11 percent. The unity of purpose offered voters, organizers, and professional Democrats a heartening sense of direction. And that passion refused to dissipate when 2005 rolled around. Having spent the election aggressively defending and advancing his foreign-policy vision, Bush was content to move on in his second term to other issues. Democrats kept their focus on the emotions and convictions that had united them, and didn't let them drop, all of which boiled down to: Bush was a liar.

That was the binding glue, and it served Democrats well as they held together to battle Bush in 2005. And God knows the Democratic Party was in desperate need of binding glue. It was especially fortunate that the binding glue came not from shared conviction about what Democrats ought to be doing but rather from a common sense of outrage at the malfeasance of the other guys—the bad guys.

———————

WHILE DEMOCRATS DEVOTED themselves to the idea that Republicans were the bad guys because of the Iraq policy, in the background there loomed a bad-guy Republican story that really did involve bad guys—and depending on its reach and extent, may be just what Democrats need to win back the House of Representatives in 2006 and give them momentum going into the 2008 election year.

The looming problem is the ongoing investigation into the

astoundingly devious GOP lobbyist Jack Abramoff, which may snare several Republican representatives and senators in what could become the most notable corruption scandal on Capitol Hill since the Abscam bribes back in 1980.

According to press reports, there are six Republican congressmen whose ties to Abramoff might get them in serious hot water. The most prominent is Tom DeLay, but the most deeply implicated appears to be Congressman Bob Ney of Ohio. Ney actually used his time on the House floor to deliver speeches in 2000 attacking a Florida businessman named Gus Boulis, who was in the midst of difficult negotiations with Abramoff over the price of a casino-boat company. "There are a few bad apples out there who don't play by the rules and that is just plain wrong," Ney said about legal casino gambling. "One such example is the case of SunCruz casinos based out of Florida. Florida authorities . . . have repeatedly reprimanded SunCruz casinos and its owner Gus Boulis for taking illegal bets, not paying out their customers properly and has had to take steps to prevent SunCruz from conducting operations all together. . . . Mr. Speaker, how Sun-Cruz Casinos and Gus Boulis conduct themselves with regard to Florida laws is very unnerving."

Ney, a relatively undistinguished congressman from Ohio, never bothered to explain why he was delivering a speech about problems with a company based in Florida, more than 2,000 miles from his district. But after his peculiar floor speech, Boulis caved in to Abramoff and the two became partners, together with an Abramoff associate named Adam Kidan. Kidan became the subject of another floor speech by Ney during yet another conflict between Abramoff and the unfortunate Gus Boulis: "Since my previous statement," Ney told his colleagues in the House, who were surely not listening to a word he was saying, "I have come to learn that

SunCruz Casinos now finds itself under new ownership and, more importantly, that its new owner has a renowned reputation for honesty and integrity. The new owner, Mr. Adam Kidan . . . certainly has his hands full in his efforts to clean up SunCruz's reputation, [but] his track record as a businessman and as a citizen leads me to believe that he will easily transform SunCruz from a questionable enterprise to an upstanding establishment that the gaming community can be proud of."

Four months after Ney's unnecessary and peculiar paean to Kidan, SunCruz was in tatters, and on a February night in Fort Lauderdale, Gus Boulis's car was trapped between two others at an intersection and he was killed in a flurry of bullets. Four years after that, three reputed members of the Gambino crime family were arrested for the murder in Queens, New York. And it turned out that in the months before the hit, one of the three mobsters had been put on the payroll of the casino-boat company by none other than Ney's hero, Adam Kidan.[6]

What began as an investigation into Abramoff's double-dealing with Indian tribes—in which he took huge sums of money from one tribe wanting to build a casino and then from another tribe trying to block the first one from building that casino—turned into something far more awful. Abramoff was the most highly paid lobbyist in history. Now it turns out he got himself involved in a business transaction that probably led to a man being assassinated on a Fort Lauderdale street for the crime of having involved himself with Abramoff and his partners.

And if such a man is shown to have showered his beneficence broadly upon Republican congressmen all too eager to sup at Abramoff's teat, then Democrats will have a strong issue on which to run against the Republican Party nationwide in 2006—a nonideological assault based entirely on the corruption emanating from Jack Abramoff's extremely deep pockets.

It won't be fair if the American people blame the entire Republican Party and its 232-member caucus in the House for the misbehavior of a few, but whoever said politics was fair? The Abramoff scandal represents a way out for Democrats, because attacks on the Republican caucus in the House for corruption will not seem quite as self-serving as the attacks on Bush and the Iraq policy came to seem to the American public by the end of 2005.

WHETHER THE SUBJECT is Iraq or Abramoff, the concentration on Republican evildoing will remain vitally important for Democratic pooh-bahs because it will allow them to ignore or paper over their party's astonishing ideological incoherence.

What do I mean by incoherence? Consider the Republican Party, with all its faults and foibles. In contrast to the Democrats, it's not that difficult to say what the Republican Party stands for, either for someone sympathetic to the party or for someone who dislikes it. The GOP is basically dedicated to free markets, free trade, a militarily strong America willing to act on its own if necessary, smaller government, lower taxes, and traditional values. It doesn't always act in concert with these goals, but that's politics for you.

Now, could you, could anybody, write that simple a description of what the Democratic Party stands for? I don't think so.

Does the Democratic Party stand for larger government? Yes, but only kind of. Democrats are for it, but have no argument for it. While Republicans believe that reducing the size of government will make American lives better, it's hard to

find a Democrat these days who will argue affirmatively that
increasing the size of government will lead to a distinct improvement in American lives. Democrats now just want to
spend more money, is all. They no longer promise much in
the way of a result from all that spending. A previous generation of Democratic thinkers promised that Big Government
would actually lead to the elimination of poverty and want in
America. But after this nation spent more than $2 trillion to
eliminate poverty, that idea now seems patently absurd and
naïve, especially since everybody now seems to agree that
these intransigent social problems are too endemic and deep-
rooted to be solved simply by throwing money at them.

Democrats do believe in using government to redistribute
income through a consciously confiscatory tax policy. But
there's not much evidence that the money they want to redistribute gets to people who don't have a lot. Instead, that
money seems to vanish, to be eaten up by all the middlemen
along the way. This we've all learned through decades of
wasteful government spending, and by now nobody seems
all that optimistic that Washington and state capitals know
how to redistribute income in any meaningful way. So while
Democrats love to harp on "tax cuts for the rich," that pro-
tax stance has become almost a matter of aesthetics rather
than policy—a feeling that it's just somehow gross and unattractive for some people to have so much. That is a potent
emotion and it clearly moves a great many people, but it's
no basis for an affirmative message of any kind.

As for foreign policy and military matters, Democrats
speak primarily of America's place within an international
system of organizations, treaties, and understandings. That's
all well and good. The problem is that the international system they lionize seems designed not to protect America or
advance American interests but rather to enmesh the United
States in restraints—loose ones to be sure, and seductively

comforting ones because they suggest that like cheerful infants we will be safer if we are kept under control, but restraints nonetheless.

That, too, would be fine if there were open acknowledgment of the notion that America was simply too strong, too powerful, and too overwhelming and needed to be restrained. A great many people believe this here and abroad. Indeed, it may be the idea about the United States that has the greatest popularity among elites across the world. But inside America, no major political party could say such a thing—could say that America needs to be restrained—and hope ever to be handed the reins of power by an American public. Americans believe, rightly, that this country is an unambiguous force for good in the world and is not a vicious bully, and they don't take kindly to politicians who tell them otherwise.

What about free markets? Here, too, the Democratic Party is schizophrenic. In decades past, market-bashing was part of left-liberal dogma. Markets were soul-killing. They destroyed culture. They were inherently unjust, and needed to be controlled. Democratic socialists believed in ideas like mandated "full-employment" and the nationalization of private industry, which are the very opposite of the free market. And after a while, you didn't even have to be a socialist to believe such things. Senatorial powerhouse Hubert Humphrey, the man known as Mr. Democrat, ended his career by advancing a "full-employment" bill that literally required America to maintain a 3 percent unemployment rate at all costs. That radical notion was swept aside by the Reagan wave and has never resurfaced. As for nationalization, its appeal lasted until, oh, 1993—when for what might have been the very last time, a major Democratic plan was advanced that would have placed one-seventh of the domestic economy under government control. That was Hillary Clinton's health care plan—the one that very nearly wiped out the Democratic Party in Washington. You don't hear much about nationalization anymore. We are all fans of the free market, Democrats as well as Republicans—at least rhetorically.

Democrats do, however, continue to represent the forces that stand in opposition to the unfettered free market. They are the party of environmentalism, which uses all the power of the courts and liberal legislators to block and stymie market development, especially in the realm of energy. And they are, above all, the party of tort law, in which trial lawyers attempt their own version of income redistribution by suing private companies, contractors, and anyone with insurance for malfeasance, malpractice, or a declining stock price. Republicans seek to limit the reach of tort law on the grounds that it's a terrible interference in the free market that ends up costing consumers a ridiculous amount of money and stifles innovation; Democrats oppose tort limits at all turns. But they do not do so while arguing that the free market is itself a bad thing.

And finally, there is free trade. You might expect the party that wants the United States to be a good citizen of the world, fully integrated into the international system, to support free trade on the grounds that it will help spread the wealth around the world and provide poor countries with a leg up. You might also expect the party that claims to speak for the least well-to-do among us to support the manufacture and sale of goods that can be sold at reasonable prices. Instead, the Democratic Party has increasingly become a party of protectionism, siding with the interests of the 8 percent of American workers in the private sector who are unionized rather than with the overwhelming majority of Americans who are not. And yet one of the great triumphs of the presidency of Bill Clinton was the passage of the

North American Free Trade Agreement (NAFTA), which got through Congress only because of Republican support.

In fact, the only area in which the Democratic Party appears to be united, optimistic, and ready to advance what it believes is a positive vision is in the realm of values. Here we find startling unity on social and cultural matters. Democrats now all share a deep conviction in favor of greater social openness on all fronts, which causes them to feel the need to introduce profound social change into ancient institutions. Democrats perceive conservatives as hidebound and backward-looking. Democrats believe in the vital necessity of amending marriage laws to include same-sex couples and to grant such couples the full range of rights and privileges granted traditional married couples. For them, this is a civil-rights issue no different from the effort to expand the rights of blacks, women, and the handicapped, and anyone who opposes it is prima facie a bigot, a fanatic, or a sellout to bigoted fanatics.

Except that, of course, Democratic politicians in Washington can't possibly allow themselves to support gay marriage and full rights for homosexuals when it comes time to vote on legislation. Democrats as well as Republicans supported the 1996 Defense of Marriage Act, a piece of legislation designed to make it impossible for judges to legalize gay marriage at the federal level. DOMA was signed into law by Bill Clinton. In 2004, John Kerry said he opposed gay marriage. Hillary Clinton says she opposes gay marriage. They're almost certainly lying, of course. Everything else they believe in suggests without question that they are gay-marriage supporters. They just can't say so because to do so would be politically ruinous for them when it comes to holding on to some crucial Catholic and Southern voters.

So on this one type of issue about which Democrats are

united in a positive way, they just can't come out and say so. What basis is this for a major political party?

It isn't much of one. What's happened here is nothing less than stunning. The present-day Democratic Party has become an entirely polemical and negative force. It exists to oppose. It draws all its power, energy, and strength not from its own positive agenda but rather from the active, frenetic, and enormously powerful dislike its rank-and-file members feel for Republicans and the Republican Party. What are Democrats? Democrats are *not Republicans.* Whatever Republicans are, Democrats are not. Republicans are big churchgoers? Well, then, Democrats deride faith. They say Republicans live in Jesus Land while they are far more cosmopolitan and skeptical (except for African-Americans, whose churchgoing must be respected). Republicans hunt? Democrats hate guns. Republicans are for relaxing environmental regulations? Democrats are for increasing them.

Democrats understand they have a problem. That's why they've started funding think tanks and public-policy institutes that ape the ones conservatives created in the 1970s. There's a profound difference between the situation of Democrats now and the conservative Republicans then, though. In the 1970s, conservatism had no home, no institutions, no places to develop ideas or house the thinkers who came up with those ideas. Academic conservatives were finding their campuses increasingly inhospitable to them, and they could not make a living writing articles for small magazines. These institutions were founded because there was no place where creative thinking on these matters could take place.

Democrats don't have that problem. Left-liberals hold sway in the universities and in the nonprofit sector, and both spend and receive vastly more foundation money than conservatives ever have (the yearly budget of the Ford Foundation alone is twice as large as the sums spent by all conservative foundations combined). Democrats also have in the mainstream media a ready and willing audience for their vaguest notions.

What they don't have is a unifying core of principles, and all the tenured professorships and think-tank affiliations in the world aren't going to provide them with that vital core. Ideas aren't generated by buildings or money. They emerge organically when people think hard about first principles and how to apply their core values and convictions to the knotty issues of the moment. That is what happened on the right in the 1960s and 1970s. From the neoconservatives in the cities to the New Right in the towns and suburbs, the intellectuals and grassroots leaders on the starboard side of the political divide began from two key premises: The United States is the greatest country on earth, and Communism is the most destructive force on earth. Neither of these premises was universally accepted. Indeed, they were even rather controversial (many otherwise rational people argued at the time that Sweden was the greatest country on earth, amazingly enough). But they formed the basis of everything from which contemporary conservatism has flowed.

When Democrats talk, as they do these days, about needing a "positive agenda," they are speaking from deep within a chasm. You shouldn't have to *devise* a positive agenda. You should just have one, and it should be known to all even before you put it down on paper. In the run-up to the 2006 elections, there was talk of a Democratic version of the Republican "Contract with America," the ten-point agenda for change that Newt Gingrich and his colleagues presented in the months before the 1994 election. But the Contract with America was nothing new for Republicans. Every conservative could have come up with the Gingrich list on his own off the top of his head—tax cuts, tort reform, crime reduction, family-friendly tax credits, term limits, and the like. Every single one of the ten pieces of legislation proposed in the Contract with America had been poll-tested and had received more than 70 percent support in those polls. The Contract with America was Conservative Reform Republicanism 101. The very fact that there's no clear set of policy proposals Democrats could easily pull off the shelf and package the way Gingrich and Friends did in 1994 indicates the intellectual slough of despond in which the party has become mired.

———

BUT WHILE THE Democratic Party is in the soup where ideas are concerned, its standing as the Not-Republican Party does offer it some sweet rewards—in the form of lavish funding from rich people who are willing to write large checks solely out of their disgust with Bush and the GOP. For the first time in this country's history, a gigantic amount of money is pouring out of rich men's coffers into left-wing pockets.

This wasn't supposed to happen. Democrats themselves tried to change the rules so that something like this couldn't happen, because until it happened for them, they considered such fantastic largesse the root of all evil. For a decade or more, Democrats had pushed for campaign-finance reforms designed to reduce the role of rich-guy money in politics. They got their wish when the campaign-finance bill championed by Republican John McCain and Democrat Russ Feingold finally became law in 2002. And like all such "reforms," what followed it was worse (if you think money in politics is bad, which I don't) than what had preceded it—to wit, that $200 million in independent expenditures raised by 527 groups like America Coming Together.

In the immediate aftermath of the 2004 Democratic defeat, there was chortling and glee among Republicans about how all that money had gone to absurd waste. An amusing

blog called Cold Hearted Truth even named key leftist donor
George Soros the "Loser of the Year," ahead of John Kerry,
Dan Rather, and Michael Moore:

"Soros was a guy who had one goal and one goal only in
2004: to do whatever it took to defeat George W Bush. Whatever it took this year meant donating over 26 million dollars
of his own money to various 527 groups. . . . The 527's did a
good job of raising money largely because of the huge contributions of people like Soros. They ran hard hitting (if not ob-
noxious) ads that attacked George W. Bush on almost every
issue that exists. They did it with over the top rhetoric that
was shocking and even somewhat effective at first. But as
the campaign wore on and the over the top attacks continued eventually people became weary of the apparent hate."[7]

John Kerry's loss must have been a bitter pill for George
Soros and others like him to swallow, but Soros himself said
a few months later, "I don't feel it's an investment that's
gone bad, because when you stand up for principles you have
to do it whether you win or lose. I'm distressed that Bush
was re-elected, but I don't feel that I wasted my money."[8]
Soros wasn't deluding himself. He may not have purchased
Bush's defeat, but he led the way in stimulating extraordinary voter turnout despite a completely underwhelming and
dislikable candidate. And there's no question that the efforts
of Soros and the 527s helped generate the wave of young
people who voted in 2004. That (together with the even
more impressive Republican get-out-the-vote effort) may
have been the most significant event of the 2004 election for
Democrats, because it may have led American politics to
take a new direction—from low voter turnout to exception-
ally high voter turnout. The best predictor of whether someone will vote is whether that someone has voted before, and
in 2004, 122 million people cast ballots, a little more than

60 percent of the voting-age population. We hadn't seen turnout that substantial in more than four decades.

Indeed, as liberal writer Matt Bai put it in the *New York Times Magazine,* Soros may have changed the nature of American politics forever. "Before Soros . . . plunked down all that cash for ACT, liberal donors had assumed that their only avenue into the political system was through supporting the [Democratic] party and its candidates, both of whom seemed to regard them as little more than a cash machine with some annoying voice commands," Bai wrote. Soros "showed Democrats, and more than a few Republicans, that there was a new way of doing business, and it didn't require fealty to an inefficient party apparatus. From this revelation—no matter how Congress or the Federal Elections Commission may try to yet again amend the campaign-finance rules—there is probably no going back."[9]

BAI SAYS WE HAVE entered a "post-party world." That may be stretching it. He's right that the rules of the game are changing. It appears that officials of the Democratic Party won't have total control over election-year spending aimed at getting their candidates over the top. To which I say: Big deal. Party officials are about as good at these sorts of things as any crew of hidebound bureaucrats who act like they know everything when they know precious little. And in any event, the candidates who benefit from the "post-party era" funded by Soros will still be Democrats. The expenditures may be independent. The candidacies will not be.

In 2006 and 2008, Democrats will want and need that 527 money again—including, or perhaps especially, Hillary Rodham Clinton. But it won't just automatically flow into Hillary's coffers. She and the other Democrats will have to earn it. And since the Democrats have no ideas, the best way—the only way—for them to keep the dollars flowing is to stay on the anti-Republican attack. These big-money donors aren't, if truth be told, all that interested in the specifics of a Democratic agenda. They have bought into the idea— actually, it's not really an idea, it's a feeling—that the country is being destroyed from within and the world is being destroyed from without by evil and crazed Republicans.

It's odd, really. In the 1970s and 1980s, grassroots Republicans perfected the art of raising money in amounts from $10 to $100 through the use of direct-mail packages crammed full of overripe rhetoric about the destructive monstrosity of liberals and the Democratic Party. Now those same techniques have been adapted to the Internet age, with online fundraising. But even more striking is that these extreme, amazingly unsophisticated messages have stirred donors with a great deal of money to pour millions into these efforts. Turns out there's very little difference between a little old lady writing a check to a televangelist who promises to cleanse America of its liberal sins, and Barbra Streisand plunking a cool million into some 527. Democrats used to make fun of those little old ladies, scorning them for their lack of education. Interesting to note that much of the Hollywood elite—Streisand, Spielberg, Geffen, Reiner, whoever— never went to college either.

What really gets Streisand and Co. going, what really drives them into frenzies of check-writing fury, is the Bush Doctrine. They believe that the American effort to democratize the Middle East—starting with Iraq—is either (a) a lie, (b) a failure, (c) an act of imperialist aggression, (d) a way of avenging Bush's father's 1992 defeat, (e) a way for Bush to trump his father, (f) . . . I'll tell you what, you write (f)—I'm tired already. They are certain that Bush's Middle East policy is at best a rancid failure and at worst a crime against humanity. They want American troops pulled out no matter the cost, and though they say that this is because they care about the troops, they're just lying. They want to hand Bush a defeat, period. They want him to lose, and if America loses, then that's fine too. Most of them, I'm sure, were thrilled with the idea of Congressman John Murtha's immediate pullout.

But as the 403–3 vote in the House of Representatives against the modified Murtha pullout proposal demonstrated, the elected officials in the Democratic Party don't feel they can make the journey to the far left that their donors and their voting base have made. They made the calculated decision that they could not become the party of unilateral withdrawal and national defeat.

And so here we see the fault line in the Democratic coalition. This fault line is one of the key opportunities for the effort to stop Hillary Clinton from becoming president.

———

ALL SUCCESSFUL CANDIDATES have to thread the political needle. They need to satisfy the narrow demands of their party's nominating base, which comprises a shockingly small number of people, something like 4 or 5 million at most, fewer than the number of votes cast in New York state. (Though in truth, the number is usually dramatically lower than that. In the two races that effectively won John Kerry the Democratic nomination in 2004, the Iowa caucuses and the New Hampshire primary, Kerry received the support of no more than 140,000 voters.*) The party base is inevitably more ideologically driven than Election Day voters, which means that in the GOP they will usually be more right-wing and in the Democratic Party more left-wing.

———

* Kerry scored 87,300 votes in New Hampshire, but since Iowa is a caucus state, it's very difficult to say how many actual people "stood up" (as the caucusers say) for Kerry. The best estimate seems to be around 50,000.

The problem for Hillary is this: She knows, better than anyone in her party, that any attempt to satisfy the open hunger of the party's new base by agreeing to give that base what it wants most of all—an American defeat in Iraq engineered not by Iraqi insurgents but by an American tide against the war—will kill off her hopes in a 2008 general election and do serious damage to the Democratic Party's prospects for the future.

But she can't turn on them. She can't attack them. She can't use them as her Sister Souljah. She can't stand up and say, "You are wrong on the merits. I'm proud I voted for the war and proud of our efforts." They're just too powerful, too rich, and too—what's the word I'm searching for? oh, yes—crazy.

In the early 1980s, as an economically devastated Britain handed the reins of power over to conservative Margaret Thatcher, the country's Labour Party went absolutely crackers, particularly those Labour politicians in and around London. Their advocacy of Marxist economics and an unabashedly pro-Soviet foreign policy led to the creation of an unforgettable nickname: They were "the Loony Left," and their irrational politics led to the marginalization of the Labour Party for eighteen long years.

The spirit of the "Loony Left"—in particular, its refusal to believe that the West is at war with an immensely dangerous ideological enemy and its deep conviction that America is the world's bad guy—is alive and well among the passionate and irrational donors and shock troops of the not-Republican coalition.

Call this force the "Neo-Loony Left." Its leading intellectual prophet is Noam Chomsky. Its leading propagandist is Michael Moore. Its frontline daily publication is the Huffington Post. And its undisputed leader—for a time, at least, in 2005—was Cindy Sheehan, the grieving mom who was converted by the mainstream media into the Mother Courage of Our Time.

The television newscasters and reporters who gave her the sort of coverage usually reserved for missing teenage blond girls in Aruba were determined not to notice that most of the words that came out of Sheehan's mouth were demented and offensive. She opposed the removal of al Qaeda's safe haven in Afghanistan, referred to the United States as "the biggest terrorist outfit in the world," called New Orleans in the wake of Hurricane Katrina "occupied New Orleans." She referred to President Bush, whom she had met a year earlier and praised as "a man of faith" who "feels some pain for our loss,"[10] as a "filth spewer." She spewed her own filth by offering up the classic anti-Semitic canard that "my son joined the army to protect America, not Israel." She offered the following pearl of wisdom about the twentieth century: "When I was growing up, it was Communists. Now it's terrorists. So you always have to have somebody to fight and be afraid of, so the war machine can build more bombs, guns, and bullets and everything." Sheehan enjoyed referring to people as "warmongers." She called Bush a warmonger, which is arguable. She called John McCain, a man who had his arms broken by his captors in a North Vietnamese prison and chose for inexplicable reasons of his own to meet with her, a "warmonger" too.

Yes, this was the wondrous woman who possessed "absolute moral authority," to quote a classic bit of bubble-headed inanity that spilled out from the brittle and dainty teacup in which resides the cerebrum of the *New York Times*'s Maureen Dowd.

And guess who else, according to Cindy Sheehan, is nothing less than a "warmonger"? You got it: Hillary Rodham Clinton. "I think she is a political animal who believes she has to be a war hawk to keep up with the big boys," she wrote in October 2005, in describing a meeting she and another mother of a dead American soldier had with the New York senator. "Mrs. Clinton stayed for a moment to tell us that she had met with other Gold Star Mothers who had a different view. I said that didn't really matter, because our view is the right one."[11]

The voice of "absolute moral authority" issued this dictum: "Senator Clinton: come out against this occupation of Iraq. Not because it is the politically expedient thing to do, but because it is the right thing to do. If you want to make Casey's sacrifice count, bring his buddies home alive. If you do not, like many American moms, I will resist your candidacy with every bit of my strength."

Chances are good that by the time Hillary faces primary voters in 2008, Cindy Sheehan will either be a trivia question or someone wandering around Iowa and New Hampshire looking for a reporter to talk to. But the threat represented by Sheehan's words—the threat of a concerted push against Hillary's nomination by the most passionate constituency in the not-Republican coalition—was and is not to be taken lightly. The intensity of the hatred for the war and the desire to see America humiliated on the part of the neo-crazy base cannot be ignored. A wildly overblown cover story in the *New Republic* magazine declared Hillary "the new villain of the anti-war Left," as its author, Michael Crowley, tried to make the case that Wisconsin senator Russ Feingold might represent a threat to Hillary from her left.

That would be a dream—a dream for Republicans and conservatives. There could be nothing quite so wonderful as having Russ Feingold to run against in 2008. He is one of the two or three most unambiguously left-wing politicians in the United States. He is scoring well in polls on the neo-crazy base websites MyDD.com and DailyKos.com, which is the functional equivalent of having Pat Buchanan and Pat

Robertson just nuts for you if you're a Republican. (And if you think a woman might have some difficulties becoming president, just stop for a minute and ask yourself whether a radical left-wing Jew could.)

Unfortunately, the Democrats will be too hungry to prevail in 2008 to do something so self-destructive. But the pressure exerted by the Neo-Loony Left will be a potent force in Democratic Party politics. Hillary has tried a variety of tactics to address it. Clearly aware that it would be disastrous for her credibility if she simply changed positions on the war in Iraq and became an antiwar activist, she didn't have a great many options. So the first cutesy trick she and Bill tried was to use her husband as ballast on her left flank. In (of all places) the Arab Emirate of Dubai in November 2005, the former president suddenly emerged as a critic of the war. It was, he said, "a big mistake . . . I don't agree with what was done."[12]

This was a bizarre thing for Bill to do. He had never said anything like it before. Indeed, in a long interview with *Esquire* magazine that hit newsstands at almost the same moment, Clinton defended George W. Bush's sincerity of conviction in believing the world needed Saddam Hussein gone. Even odder was the fact that only five days later, Hillary used the very same words—"a big mistake"—to describe John Murtha's notion of an immediate withdrawal from Iraq. "I think," Hillary continued, "that [an immediate pullout] would cause more problems for us in America. It will matter to us if Iraq totally collapses into civil war, if it becomes a failed state the way Afghanistan was, where terrorists are free to basically set up camp and launch attacks against us."[13]

These weren't especially controversial words, and what she said was not at all supportive of the administration. She added that the Bush policy was the result of "poor decision-making" and that it was giving the Iraqis "an open-ended invitation not to take care of themselves." Her words were echoed or duplicated by John Kerry, among others, in subsequent days. And, as we've seen, the vast majority of elected Democrats in Washington refused to endorse any policy advocating withdrawal from Iraq.

But the reaction to her anti-Murtha rhetoric was an indication that she had some trouble on her left to deal with. A diarist on DailyKos.com, the minute-by-minute website by and for the Neo-Loons, issued this warning: "Hillary, you have until December 1 [2005] to voice your opinion that you made the wrong decision here. It's not like this would be politically risky, either locally or nationally. Everyone's doing it! Are you going to be able to admit a mistake and show strength, or will I have to abstain [in voting for her reelection in New York] come next November?"14

Earlier in the year, Neo-Loons had spoken primarily in tones of sorrow rather than anger about some of Hillary's choices. When she appeared at the annual meeting of the centrist Democratic Leadership Council in July 2005 and called for an ideological truce inside the Democratic Party—"we Democrats have not yet succeeded in isolating and defeating the far right," she said, "in part because we have allowed ourselves to be split between left, right, and center"15—she received a grumpy reception from the Neo-Loons. Markos Moulitsas, the man behind DailyKos.com, wrote, "It's truly disappointing that this is the crap Hillary has signed on to. More of the failed corporatist bullshit that has cost our party so dearly the last decade and a half."16

There was precious little sorrow and more than a little anger when DailyKos's December 1 deadline came and went without a satisfactory change of position from Hillary. Perhaps the pithiest expression of discontent came from the always delightful Tim Robbins, the Oscar-winning actor whose talent for playing nincompoops onscreen is dwarfed by his

talent for simply being a nincompoop in real life. Robbins
went on Air America Radio's morning show on December 1
and sputtered, "Hillary Clinton can kiss my butt."

Robbins was not only angry at her unwillingness to advocate a cut-and-run strategy in Iraq, he was also peeved at the
text of a letter she released in the last week of November attempting to quiet down the anger she was provoking on the
Neo-Loony Left.

It was an extraordinary document—1,600 words of self-
justification. Though Hillary said in the letter that she
"take[s] responsibility for her vote . . . to authorize the Administration to use force in Iraq," in fact the whole point of
her missive was to deny any such responsibility. Rather, the
onus was on the administration's supposed mendacity and
knowing, conscious misdeeds: "I voted for it on the basis of
the evidence presented by the Administration, assurances
they gave that they would first seek to resolve the issue
of weapons of mass destruction peacefully through United
Nations sponsored inspections, and the argument that the
resolution was needed because Saddam Hussein never did
anything to comply with his obligations that he was not
forced to do. Their assurances turned out to be empty ones,
as the Administration refused repeated requests from the
U.N. inspectors to finish their work. And the 'evidence' of
weapons of mass destruction and links to al Qaeda turned
out to be false."[17]

There's no point in arguing with the statements in the letter. It deconstructed itself sentence by sentence. The war
should never have taken place, she said, but she was not to
be faulted for supporting it: "Based on the information that
we have today, Congress never would have been asked to
give the President authority to use force against Iraq. And if
Congress had been asked, based on what we know now, we

never would have agreed, given the lack of a long-term plan, paltry international support, the proven absence of weapons of mass destruction, and the reallocation of troops and resources that might have been used in Afghanistan to eliminate bin Laden and al Qaeda, and fully uproot the Taliban." In other words, since both president and Congress had the same information, Bush should have had perfect foresight, but nobody could expect that of Hillary or her fellow senators who voted for the war.

Hillary was trying to send a message to the Neo-Loony Left: she was paying close attention to its screeches and was eager to find some sort of common ground with it. The letter was a gesture of respect, a bow of obeisance to its central role in the politics of the present moment. It was, therefore, an important early play in her presidential bid.

And the failure of the letter to calm the Neo-Loons was instructive. Since she is running for president, it is in the self-interest of every Democratic Party faction not to waltz right into her arms and sing hosanna. They need to put her on notice that they are not pushovers, because if she can simply count on their support, she can spend her time and energy doing things to please some other constituency. Like Glenn Close in *Fatal Attraction*, they "won't be ignored," and yelling at Hillary is the political version of boiling her bunny to get her attention.

They have surely gotten it. Hillary's strategy over the next couple of years will follow along these lines. She will want to harness the Left's enthusiasm and its money, and keep it happy—or if not happy, then at least not in open revolt against her. She needs the Neo-Loony Left to believe that she represents her party's best hope for victory against the evildoing Republicans. But she also needs the Neo-Loons to understand that only by appearing to ignore them she can beat the monsters on the right. She will wink at the Left in every way possible, hinting that she will try to satisfy their desires once the presidency is secured.

Hillary will, therefore, be implicitly pursuing the same strategy proposed, in the most vulgar but revealing possible fashion, by Democratic Congressman Peter Kostmayer during Michael Dukakis's unsuccessful bid for the presidency in 1988. "We're not going to blow it this time," Kostmayer said. "Just shut up, gays, women, and environmentalists. Just shut up. You'll get everything you want after the election. But just, for the meantime, shut up so that we can win."[18]

Conservatives can't allow her to get away with it.

———

IS IT FAIR to assume, as I do, that in her heart of hearts, Hillary Clinton's deepest and truest sympathies lie with the Neo-Loony Left? That, having consciously positioned herself as a centrist Democrat, she would as president govern as a left-liberal? After all, it was Hillary who helped design Bill's move to the center after he was kicked out of the Arkansas governor's mansion in 1980 by bringing in the brilliantly elastic consultant Dick Morris to help reframe her husband's political career and move him rightward.

Morris has no doubts. The consultant, whose love-hate relationship with Bill Clinton has since been supplanted by his hate-hate relationship with Hillary, says flatly that "Hillary Clinton would be the most liberal president we've had since Lyndon Johnson"[19]—a frightening thought, considering that Jimmy Carter spent four years in the White House swinging a leftist wrecking ball across the United States.

To be reminded of Hillary's liberal sympathies, you need to look no further than her voting record in the Senate on every issue save the war in Iraq. Clearly, she has made a self-conscious effort in her public statements to appear to be a centrist. But we have little reason, when we consider her votes, to believe that such efforts would continue in the presidency.

The only way to find out the answer for sure, of course, would be to elect her president. And the truth is that the stakes are simply too high for that. The rantings of Cindy Sheehan and DailyKos.com should be enough to convince anyone who isn't consumed by a desire to see the United States defeated in the War on Terror that allowing such people and their ideas anywhere near the White House would be a catastrophic mistake. The enhanced power of the Neo-Loony Left, its capacity to raise money and to do grassroots organizing, means that it will play a substantial role in the 2008 election—and if it contributes to a Democratic victory, it will be due some of the spoils of that victory.

And so here we come to the basis of the plan I'm proposing—the plan to stop Hillary Clinton.

The plan calls for exploiting the tension between what the Neo-Loons want—a frankly leftist Democratic candidate who will reverse field and drastically change the policies of the U.S. government in the war against Islamofascism and the domestic war on terror—and what it will take to win a national election in November 2008.

Hillary's aim will be to finesse the gap between the primary Democrats and the electorate—to make it appear that her nomination is unstoppable and therefore that it would be suicidal for anyone who wants the Republicans to lose to work at cross-purposes with her. She and her people will trumpet the vast sums of money she will have in the bank at the beginning of the race to frighten competitors away. She will line up endorsements of major officials across the country as early as possible. She will attempt to create the air of inevitability in hopes that it will tame those on her left flank.

To that end, she will use all the tools that have worked well for her as an office seeker and an elected politician. In particular, she will retreat into silence when it comes to advancing the details of her own agenda, and will continue to speak out in general but hardly meaningful terms against Bush and the Republicans. She will want to glide into her party's nomination if at all possible to give her every possible option on how to approach winning the election.

It will be up to her Republican opponents to see that, as Kostmayer might have said, she isn't able to just shut up. In an odd way, Republicans should stand shoulder to shoulder with the Neo-Loons. Like the Neo-Loons, we must demand that Hillary show herself. It must be our goal to compel her to take a leadership role in her party at the earliest possible moment.

What we want is for Hillary to become a political warrior, to become the voice and face of her party by the beginning of 2007. We want her standing at the ramparts, raising high the flag of the Not-Republican Party. We want her to feel obliged to lead attempted filibusters in the Senate against Bush nominees and Bush legislation. We want her to vote against Bush judges and to make long speeches and media appearances about her votes. And because she is evidently certain she cannot afford to renounce her own votes on the Bush wars, we want her to become even more hot and bothered about every aspect of the implementation of those conflicts for which she voted.

This is our best hope. If she takes up the cudgels of her radicalized party in order to secure the nomination, she will have to place herself foursquare in the liberal camp in such a decisive way that she will not be able to tack to the center so easily. If she fails to do so, she will create an opportunity for other Democrats eager to be president to come at her for her cowardice and lack of principle, and use that argument to stage a serious and possibly successful effort to seize the nomination from her.

And the good news is, Republicans and conservatives have the means, the motive, and the opportunity to make it happen. All you need do is follow my ten-point plan.

Interested? Well, join me, won't you . . .

Part III

"STOP HILLARY": THE TEN-POINT PLAN

So here we are. The Republican Party is divided and troubled, with various portents of gloom and potential swords of doom hanging over its head. But it is still the wellspring of positive ideas about how to move the country forward and make the world a better place—and it holds the whip hand in Washington. The Democratic Party is resurgent, full of beans, with a charged-up base and a list of donors willing to shower hundreds of millions of dollars on its efforts to dethrone the Republicans. But the Democrats don't know

what they stand for and cannot come up with a single unifying principle other than distaste for the GOP.

Still, if you had to bet on who the next president will be,
right now the safest bet would be Hillary. This is true despite the fact that the most passionate and active members
of the left-liberal coalition have grown suspicious of her, in
spite of the sense among Democrats in the 1990s that she
was the most reliable advocate of leftist causes inside the
Clinton White House.

To stop her, Republicans will have to try to exploit her
weaknesses and those of her party, while playing to their
own strengths and trying to neutralize some of their party's
shortcomings. The goal is to try to get Hillary and the
Democrats to *make mistakes* while trying your damnedest
to keep from making too many on your own.

The 2008 election is without precedent in the modern
media age. For the first time since 1952, as I've said, America will have a wide-open race for the presidency, with neither a sitting president seeking reelection nor a sitting vice
president trying to fill his boss's seat. That's fourteen elections without a candidate certain in the race. That's fifty-six
years. Kind of stunning, when you think about it—so stunning that anything could happen.

Republicans will lose if they do not stand firm on the
ground that has supported them and the party for more than
twenty-five years—a strong military, an aggressive foreign
policy that promotes democratic change, support for traditional values, limited government, and low taxes. Any candidate who can make it through the bruising nomination
process while holding firm to these precepts can win. A candidate who tries to get himself elected without these pillars
supporting his candidacy can't.

The ten-point "Stop Hillary" plan combines strategic
thinking, policy proposals, and a specific suggestion about

which specific candidate I think could do the best job of stopping her and keeping the presidency in Republican hands. But the plan doesn't rely on the GOP going with my choice, and it shouldn't. Like all presidential elections, this one will be about ideas and about vision—about how the candidates see the future of America and the world.

In order to win, Republicans need to expose the inconsistencies in Hillary's ideas and her lack of vision, while avoiding the unforced errors that will give Hillary a chance to focus voter attention on the troubling aspects of Republican leadership. I don't pretend to believe that the failure to follow my plan will mean Republicans will lose in 2008. But I hope my plan will serve as food for thought for those who actually have to go out and win this thing.

SMOKE HER OUT

By far the greatest weapon in Hillary's arsenal is her undisputed standing as the most famous person in American politics who is not now nor has ever been president. Her stardom affords her privileges other politicians lack—among them, the ability to pick and choose the moments at which she takes center stage. Other politicians fight for the spotlight, but since Hillary can have it whenever she wants it, she uses it carefully.

In 2005, for example, she gave only 11 speeches on the floor of the Senate. By contrast, Joseph Biden, the Delaware Democrat, gave 37 speeches. Hillary's official website lists an astonishingly small number of public statements for a public official during her Senate career—a mere 87 in five years' time, and at least a third of those weren't delivered before her fellow senators. I'm not saying she has been entirely mute. She serves on committees, those committees hold hearings, and she asks questions during those hearings. But like a stealth bomber, she maintains radio silence for long periods of time.

Her parsimony when it comes to telling people just where she stands is one of the reasons that she has come to be perceived, falsely, as a "moderate" or a "centrist" in the Senate. For the years 2004 and 2005, according to the Lexis-Nexis database, she was described as "moderate" in the media an astonishing 119 times and as a "centrist" 61 times—even though she holds a 96 percent liberal rating from the venerable Americans for Democratic Action. The ADA's sine qua non liberal rating is based on actual voting records in the Senate. The only reason she did not get a perfect liberal score in 2004 is that she voted against a ban on missile-defense testing. On every other matter, from social issues like abortion to pocketbook issues like tax cuts, she toed the liberal line.

As I've said, her reputation for moderation is based almost entirely on the fact that she voted for the war with Iraq and for subsequent defense appropriations. And every now and then she will go for the kind of gimmick her husband (under Dick Morris's tutelage) used to specialize in—a pointless crusade against a social ill for the purpose of convincing voters who aren't paying much attention that she has some conservative tendencies. She joined with conservative Democratic Senator Joseph Lieberman in a crusade against violent and overly sexual video games, for example. "I have developed legislation," she announced in November 2005, "that will empower parents by making sure their kids can't walk into a store and buy a video game that has graphic, violent and pornographic content."[1]

A week after that, she announced she would, along with conservative Republican senator Robert Bennett of Utah, cosponsor a law to outlaw flag-burning. According to this surpassingly silly piece of legislation, it would be illegal to "intimidate" anyone by burning a flag, or to burn a flag on federal property, or to burn a flag owned by someone else. The "intimidation" standard would be impossible to prove or disprove in court. If it is legal to burn a flag as a free-speech statement, a court would surely find it is legal to do so on federal property. And it goes without saying that it's already a crime to burn a flag that doesn't belong to you.

No matter. By putting herself forward, Hillary got the news stories she wanted for legislative initiatives that will almost certainly never see the light of day—a prime example of how she uses her fame to pick and choose her subjects. She speaks only rarely on hot-button issues like abortion, where she plays a familiar cutesy game. In the Senate, she votes against any conceivable restriction on abortion rights and votes against judges who are not pro-choice. But when she speaks, she plays the moderate card, complaining about Chinese and Romanian forced birth-control practices and asserting, as she did in January 2005, "There is no reason why government cannot do more to educate and inform and provide assistance so that the choice guaranteed under our constitution either does not ever have to be exercised or only in very rare circumstances."[2]

Her effort to have it every which way on Iraq was another example. "I do not believe we have an easy choice here," she said in early December 2005. "I disagree with those who believe we should pull out, and I disagree with those who believe we should stay without end."[3]

This was an odd formulation, since there is no one on earth who "believes we should stay without end." But forced into making statements about Iraq, Hillary had to find a way to appear to separate herself from the Bush administration while not changing sides.

She would have been better off maintaining the silence that has served her so effectively over the years. But on Iraq, the political crisis created in the late fall of 2005 by the division in the Democratic Party made silence impossible—and her effort to square the circle and find a slick-as-Willie way out of it shows how Hillary can do herself real damage when she's forced (as my Yiddish-speaking grandmother would have said) to open a mouth.

No more silence from Hillary. She cannot be allowed to isolate herself in the mansion of her own mind.

Republicans must smoke her out. With Hillary as the

2008 frontrunner, Republicans must now—right now, this week, today—declare her the leader of the Democratic Party and insist that she become its primary voice and its primary spokesman.

This should be our cry: "We want to hear from Hillary." On blogs and radio shows, in letters to the editor and op-eds in newspapers, and in communications with reporters, we should insist on "hearing from Hillary."

We should say, "Enough blather from Howard Dean, the nominal chairman of the Democratic National Committee. Enough silliness emanating from the mouth of Nancy Pelosi, the House minority leader, who found it too difficult from week to week to decide whether she was for an immediate pullout from Iraq or a partial pullout or an 'Extreme Makeover: Iraq Edition.' No more meaningless talk from Harry Reid, the Senate minority leader, which makes him a leader only in his own mind. Who cares what has-beens like Teddy Kennedy and Robert Byrd have to say? America wants to hear from Hillary."

If a controversy erupts on a matter having to do with, say, Iraq, or the Patriot Act, or taxes, or entitlements, or out-of-control government spending, or North Korea, or Iran, or the highway bill, or tort reform, or a car-company bailout, or airline bankruptcies, or the misbehavior of Venezuelan strongman Hugo Chávez, or the United Nations oil-for-food scandal, or the avian flu, or disaster management—basically, any question that a president or a presidential candidate must address—the cry must go forth:

"We want to hear from Hillary."

She must go on record. Republican pundits who go on television should express their disappointment with Hillary's refusal to speak out on this or that or the other issue. Radio talk-show hosts should run clips of George W. Bush or other

Republicans talking about the issue of the day and then run a few seconds of silence to indicate that Hillary failed to address it.

And, of course, there are the blogs. Different political blogs on the right tend to become interested in specific issues—for example, Powerlineblog.com is outspoken on Israel-Palestine matters, HughHewitt.com does yeoman work on faith-related matters, JustOneMinute.typepad.com is a clearinghouse for information about CIA misconduct toward the Bush administration, and so on.

When their issue takes center stage and Hillary has not yet spoken about it, they should run a Countdown feature noting the number of days Hillary has been silent. The Countdown feature was used to great effect during the 2004 presidential election after John Kerry promised to release his military records and then just wouldn't do it. PoliPundit.com simply counted off every day that followed Kerry's unfulfilled promise. This kept the matter in the forefront of the consciousness of the blog's readers and was a constant distraction and irritant to the Kerry campaign.

This is one aspect of the Stop Hillary campaign where Republicans and conservatives can expect full help and support from the mainstream media. They may want to help get Hillary elected, but they are deeply annoyed when somebody doesn't answer questions or phone calls or make statements when statements are requested. The conservative pressure to smoke her out will excite the media, which would love to jump on the story of this epoch-making campaign as early as possible.

Smoking Hillary out will have two salutary consequences:

First, though it may seem to elevate her standing and thereby give her a helping hand toward the nomination, it will also deglamorize her. Her silence, should it continue, will call into question just how forthright she might be and whether her selective eloquence is really just rank political cowardice.

Second, it will require her and the Democratic Party she will lead to speak about what they actually intend to do should they acquire the White House—not in boring policy papers that no one will read and that can be ignored once an election takes place, but in real-time spoken words. Those words put her on record and on notice. Once spoken, they cannot be retracted. Once Hillary makes a pronouncement, she cannot pretend she never said it.

And a transparent Hillary is probably an unelectable Hillary.

MAKE HER VOTE

Hillary Clinton will win her second term as a senator from New York in November 2006. So she will run for president as an active member of the World's Greatest Deliberative Body. By choosing to campaign for president while remaining on her Senate perch, Hillary has done something she almost never has before: She's taken a chance. It would almost certainly have been the safer course to retire from the Senate in order to make her play for the White House. The statistics on senators running for president are pretty bleak. Only two sitting senators are among America's presidents. The last was John F. Kennedy nearly a half-century ago (his predecessor was Warren G. Harding in 1920).* Since Kennedy's victory, fifty-two sitting senators have sought the job. Of those fifty-two, only two—Bob Dole in 1996 and John Kerry in 2004—became their party's nominee.

And you know what happened to them.

Senators find it almost impossible to win the presidency for a very good reason, especially in the modern era: A senator casts between 200 and 500 votes a year.[1] These votes concern proposed laws at various stages in the law's development, and because of quirky procedural games, senators will often find themselves casting completely contradictory

---

* Thirteen others became president after having served in the Senate at some point in their careers.

votes on the same piece of legislation. Sometimes they are forced to do this because of vague language in the bill, or as a way of getting rid of one bill so that another one more congruent with their views can be submitted in its place.

And sometimes they do this so that they can cover all bases and claim to have voted on all sides of an issue. The most notorious recent example—perhaps the most notorious example in Senate history—had to do with John Kerry's conduct relating to a Senate bill on Iraq. At a campaign stop in West Virginia in March 2004, according to *Newsweek*, "a heckler kept demanding to know why he had voted against more funding for the troops. In his considered but long-winded fashion, Kerry tried to explain that he had wanted to vote for the funding, but only if the Senate passed an amendment that would whittle down President Bush's earlier tax cut for the rich. Kerry voted for the amendment, but when it failed, he voted against the funding. The heckler pressed, and Kerry, losing patience, fell into senatorial procedural shorthand. 'I actually did vote for the $87 billion before I voted against it,' he said."[2]

For Kerry, the controversy must have seemed baffling at first—after all, he'd been in the Senate for nineteen years, and casting votes for and against the same bill is standard, if repulsively slippery, practice there. But his throwaway remark in West Virginia was, in the words of Karl Rove, "the gift that kept on giving"[3]—the key element in the Bush campaign's effort to paint Kerry as a flip-flopper with no fixed beliefs or convictions on any matter. Remember that Kerry's vote-not-vote on the $87 billion came in 2003. Had he retired from the Senate at the beginning of the 108th Congress that year, he would not have had to cast that vote, or indeed any vote on any matter of controversy that year or in 2004. He could have refined his position to a fare-thee-well without having to go on record specifically advocating or rejecting legislation.

Kerry had troubles with his candidacy for another Senate-related reason as well: The Senate has to vote frequently when it is in session. And since Senate rules provide for "unlimited debate"—meaning that any senator can hold up a vote on any piece of legislation for as long as he likes simply by prolonging discussion of it—any member who has other obligations outside Washington is going to miss a vote here and there. For the most part, these missed votes don't matter, because if a bill passes a vote called "cloture"—a move to end the unlimited debate, which must be accepted by a three-fifths "supermajority"—it is almost bound to pass.

Usually senators are careful not to miss votes in the years before their reelection campaigns, because there's no easier or more potent issue for a rival candidate to jump on than a record of missed votes. It makes the senator in question look like a lazy bum who isn't doing his job. In 1976, running for Senate in New York against Republican James Buckley, the ultimately victorious Pat Moynihan made mincemeat of Buckley's voting record because his rival had been present only 52 percent of the time in the preceding two years.[4] Buckley protested that he had had pneumonia, but no matter—in the eyes of voters, being a senator was his job and he hadn't been doing it.

Kerry likewise came under harsh criticism in 2003 and 2004 because, as a presidential candidate, he was hardly to be seen in Washington. He was crisscrossing Iowa and New Hampshire, eating fried Twinkies and rubber chicken dinners and shaking hands until his palms bled. This meant that in 2003, according to *Congressional Quarterly*, Kerry missed an astonishing 64 percent of the Senate's votes, and the percentage was even higher in 2004 (halfway through the year, he'd skipped 89 percent of the 132 votes cast).[5] This was not only fodder for Republicans, who called Kerry's absences to the attention of reporters at every turn, but a profound irritant to Democratic interest groups as well. In May 2004, an effort by Democrats to extend unemployment benefits lost in the Senate by a single vote—John Kerry's vote. Kerry was off campaigning in Kentucky that day.[6]

So rattled was Kerry by the anger of Democrats at his missed vote that five weeks later he blew off campaign stops in New Mexico to return to Washington in the middle of the night so he could cast a vote on veterans' health care benefits—whereupon canny Republicans decided to deny Kerry his grandstanding moment. Senate Majority Leader Bill Frist, a Republican, refused to call a vote on the matter that day. "Senator Kerry, who hadn't been here all year, who's missed 80 percent of all votes," Frist said archly, "parachutes in for a day and then will be taking off once again."[7]

Why is Hillary risking this kind of unnecessary trouble by running for reelection to the Senate when she knows she's going to turn around and run for the presidency? Simple answer: Money. As I've noted previously, she can expect to raise anywhere between $50 and $100 million for her Senate race. But because her reelection is a sure thing, and because New York's state Republican Party is a colossal joke, she will only have to spend $10 million or $15 million max on her 2006 race. Every other cent she raises can be transferred into her presidential-campaign coffers—thus giving her a huge leg up on any other Democrat tempted to challenge her for the nomination.

In addition, everyone who gave her $2,000 for her Senate race can turn around and give her another $2,000 for her presidential race. It's fair to assume that most people who can afford to donate two grand to a political candidate can probably afford to donate four grand all told. Thus, she will not be cannibalizing the monetary support she will need in 2008. She will simply be doubling it.

Well, that's very nice for her, and she should only enjoy

having nice, fat coffers full of cash. But Republicans can and should and must make her pay for her decision to stay in the Senate, and turn that decision to their advantage as much as possible. She wants to be a senator running for president? Well, then, that is what she will be—with all the pain, awkwardness, and difficulty that will entail.

***

THE REPUBLICAN ADVANTAGE can be both procedural and ideological, and should follow along the smoke-her-out path outlined in Point #1. For it is not only in public statements and public appearances that Hillary can and must be compelled to go on record on matters of controversy where she would prefer to remain silent.

Because she has chosen to remain in the Senate, she can be forced to cast votes on these matters as well.

Since the ultimate priority of Republicans should be stopping Hillary, one of the priorities of Republicans in the Senate should be to use their power to make her vote. Such votes don't have to be on full pieces of legislation that must then be harmonized with comparable legislation in the House. They can merely be votes on so-called Sense of the Senate resolutions, which are not binding but can be added to existing pieces of legislation or brought up for a vote on their own. They exist to express the opinion of the Senate (the House of Representatives can do its own version) on any matter without that opinion being given the force of law. (The most notable Sense of the Senate resolution in 2005 came when Republicans foolishly decided to try to trump a Democratic call for a specific withdrawal timetable from Iraq with a milder version of it—an act that nonetheless embarrassed George W. Bush and helped create momentum for the crisis that erupted over Congressman John Murtha's call for immediate withdrawal.)

What should these Sense of the Senate resolutions aimed

at Hillary be about? You name it, just so long as it's conservative and popular and will also give liberals conniptions. Here are just a few ideas to offer a sense of how to do what I'm talking about:

- A resolution affirming the rights of parents to make decisions in the best interests of their children—which will be read as an attack on the pro-choice movement.

- A resolution affirming the rights of hunters—which will be seen as a slap at gun-control advocates.

- A resolution asserting that no locality should have the power to seize private property through the power of eminent domain solely for the purpose of economic development—which is a slap at a recent Supreme Court decision that is particularly beloved by liberals for reasons that escape me.

The goal is to get Hillary to cast ideological votes—or to increase the number of possible votes in 2007 and 2008 to such a degree that she will end up with a lousy attendance sheet.

If she continues to cast votes that retain her 96 percent liberal voting record, that will be useful fodder indeed for Republicans trying to keep her out of the White House. Remember that while liberal politicians, interest groups, and voting blocs are indeed resurgent, people really don't like to describe themselves as "liberal"—but have no problem whatever with the word *conservative*. In the bipartisan Battleground poll taken in November 2005, conducted jointly by Republican Ed Goeas and Democrat Celinda Lake, 61 percent of the respondents described themselves as "conservative" or "very conservative," while only 35 percent said they were "somewhat liberal" or "very liberal."[8]

Republicans in 2004 made great use of the fact that *National Journal*, a nonpartisan Washington publication, listed John Kerry as the "most liberal" member of the Senate in 2003 and his running mate, John Edwards, as the fourth "most liberal." The citation of the *National Journal* stat— which picks out the most ideologically charged votes cast in the Senate in any given year to make its determination— enraged Bob Somerby. He writes the Daily Howler, perhaps the most interesting of the left-leaning blogs. "That rating," the Howler howled, "is based on calendar year 2003, when both senators—campaigning for the White House—missed large numbers of the 62 votes the *Journal* used for its tabulations. (Kerry missed 37 of the 62 votes; Edwards missed 22.)"[9]

Yes! Exactly! Maybe Somerby was right that these rankings weren't entirely just, but Kerry knew what he was doing. Kerry missed a lot of these votes, but he made sure he was there for the ones that meant the most to those Democrats who make up the majority of those attending the nominating caucuses and primaries—a group that tends to be far more liberal than the population as a whole. Hillary may have to follow in Kerry's footsteps, staying out of town to do her campaign work and flying back in to make sure she votes "yea" on the heart's desires of the party Left or "nay" on the anathematic desires of the Republicans.

And maybe, just maybe, Hillary will find herself where Kerry was—both atop the *National Journal*'s list of the most liberal senators and at the top of the list of those who miss Senate votes. Assuming that Republicans maintain their majority control of the Senate in the 2006 elections, they can do quite a bit to impede her efforts to move back into her one-time residence across from Lafayette Park.

MAKE HER CRITICIZE TAX CUTS

You can date precisely the moment at which the U.S. economy turned around and began its remarkable ascent after the recession of 2001, the 9/11 attacks, and the subsequent economic doldrums. The date is May 23, 2003, when the second round of Bush tax cuts was enacted. In the third quarter of 2003, the economy grew more than 7 percent, and in the eight succeeding quarters its growth was at 3.5 percent or higher. Because economic growth was so strong, receipts to the federal government grew to the highest level in history even though taxes had been dramatically slashed—a complete vindication of the argument that tax cuts cause economic growth that in turn fills government coffers in the least painful way possible for taxpayers. The stunning Treasury Department chart on the opposite page tells it all.[1]

What this chart records is inarguable economic fact. And yet Democrats remain implacably opposed to the Bush tax cuts, all of which were designed to be "phased out"—a euphemism for "come to an end"—unless Congress acts to extend them.

Many conservatives are enraged by Congress's inability or refusal to come together to make the tax cuts permanent—in part because that can have a deleterious impact on those trying to make economic plans in the long term. In 2005, the White House sought a measure to extend the tax cut

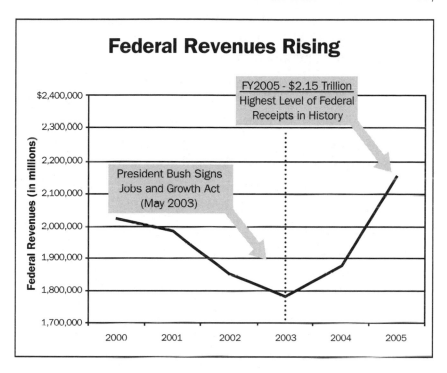

Federal Revenues Rising

FY2005 - $2.15 Trillion
Highest Level of Federal
Receipts in History

President Bush Signs
Jobs and Growth Act
(May 2003)

Federal Revenues (in millions)

on dividends and on capital gains, due to expire in 2009, through 2010. Democrats, including Hillary Clinton, were almost unanimously opposed. She has spent her Senate career criticizing the Bush tax cuts at every turn, often using the clever tack of pointing out that even though she benefits from them, she thinks they're wrong and immoral. On September 7, 2005, making the rounds of the morning chat shows, she was asked by NBC's Matt Lauer where the money to rebuild New Orleans might be coming from. She responded, "It comes from the first instance in not making those tax cuts for rich people like us permanent."[2]

That same morning, she appeared on ABC's *Good Morning America* and said, "It's been tough these last few years. The primary priority of this administration domestically has been tax cuts. And when tax cuts for the wealthiest people in the country takes priority over everything, you're going to see some effects of that over the long run. And, you know,

Charlie, that's one of my larger concerns, is that we need to put the American people first."[3]

Hillary spoke these words at a time when the American public had not yet taken the full measure of the economic boom. If that boom isn't somehow cut short, her words and her votes should be thrown back at her in the form of an advertising campaign in 2007—perhaps sponsored by the Republican version of one of those notorious 527s that raised more than $200 million for Democrats in 2004 (for Republicans are playing catch-up in the 527 world).

Even though Democrats have never really met a tax cut they didn't oppose, they really don't like to be called on it and often will gin up some itsy-bitsy measure that will allow them to claim the mantle of a tax-cutter. The anti-Hillary commercial campaign can forestall or neutralize any such effort on her part by saying as much: "When she runs for president, Hillary Clinton will tell you she wants to cut taxes. She may even throw out something that the media will call a tax cut. But the truth is, if she gets her way, if you're in the middle class, your federal taxes will be higher in three years than they are now."

How will this be so? Simple. The major element of the Bush tax cuts was a reduction in overall tax rates. Right now there are six tax brackets—35, 33, 28, 25, 15, and 10 percent. The law establishing those brackets is due to expire in 2010. If a new law is not written and passed extending those brackets, tax rates will bounce back to where they were in 2001—to 39.6, 36, 31, 28, and 15 percent.

Forget the highest tax bracket for a moment. A middle-class taxpayer now in the 25 percent bracket would find himself paying a top rate of 28 or 31 percent. A taxpayer in the 28 percent bracket would find his top rate rising to either 31 or 36 percent. And the poorest taxpayer would find his taxes increased 50 percent (from 10 to 15 percent).

The complex politics of the year 2000 forced Bush and the Republicans to design their tax cuts to "sunset" in this way absent serious action on the part of Congress and the president. And it turns out that the "sunset" clause may have been the political gift that will keep on giving (just as John Kerry's "87 billion" quote was in the last election). Republicans can let the debate over the tax brackets slide until 2008—and then strike, and strike big with a package that not only extends the tax cuts but maybe cuts rates a bit more. Democrats have made such a show of their hatred of the Bush tax cuts that it will seem hypocritical at best for them to flip-flop and support an extension. But if they *don't*, they will be on record supporting effective tax increases as large as 50 percent.

Now let's go back to the tax cuts Democrats feel that they have no difficulty opposing—the taxes that fall on the "rich," which is to say, those in the top bracket. They would argue that returning the top bracket to its pre-2001 level of 39.6 percent is a matter of simple fairness, as is eliminating the tax cuts on dividends and capital gains. On a trip to San Francisco in 2004, Hillary described her hunger to raise taxes on people like herself: "Many of you are well enough off that . . . the tax cuts may have helped you. We're saying that for America to get back on track, we're probably going to cut that short and not give it to you. We're going to take things away from you on behalf of the common good."[4]

I don't mean to be rude to Hillary Clinton, but I really don't think her idea of the "common good" is the same as mine, and therefore I would prefer that she not "take things away from" me to satisfy her own eleemosynary ambitions. I'm absolutely delighted that she said what she said, however. That phrase—"We're going to take things away from you on behalf of the common good"—is pure gold for Republicans. It could have been the 2008 version of "I actually did

vote for the $87 billion before I voted against it," except that when 2008 rolls around, the quote will be four years old. It will be useful, just not the knockout punch it would have been earlier.

Politically, the "tax the rich" stuff may seem like winning material for Democrats, but dig a little deeper and you might come to have a different view. The tax increases created by the elimination of Bush tax cuts on dividends and capital gains would fall heavily on the rich, who are not large enough in numbers to matter. But raising taxes on dividends does affect a rather sizable part of the electorate. That would be the retired elderly, part of whose fixed income derives from dividends. There are a lot of elderly people in Florida, as you may know. Those dividend tax cuts are an important reason why George W. Bush's margin of victory in Florida, with its gold mine of 27 electoral votes, rose from 930 in 2000 to 380,000 in 2004.

The Republican path to victory depends on victory in Florida. Democratic hopes for victory rely to some degree on taking Florida away from Republicans. If the GOP does its job, by Election Day 2008 there shouldn't be a person on a golf course, in a condominium community, or eating an early-bird special who doesn't know that Hillary wants to raise his taxes.

TALK UP FREE TRADE

One of the signal accomplishments of the Clinton administration was its aggressive push to secure passage of the North American Free Trade Agreement in 1993. NAFTA remains the cornerstone and the model for those who believe that free trade is simultaneously the best economic policy and the best foreign policy for the United States to pursue now and in the future. Free trade is, like all freedoms—freedom of speech, freedom of assembly, freedom of religion—the greatest bulwark against the unreasonable expansion of government power. When nations practice free trade, an organic alliance of consumers and producers functions as a check against politicians using their law-writing powers to control a marketplace they usually do not understand.

NAFTA became law despite violent opposition from important Democratic Party interest groups. Despite its importance to the newly elected Democratic president, two senior Democratic leaders in the House of Representatives, Dick Gephardt and David Bonior, fought against it. Only 42 percent of the Democrats in the House at the time voted for NAFTA. The bill passed only because 71 percent of the Republicans in Congress supported it. Even now, Democrats love to celebrate the nation's economic success during the Clinton years, but they remain silent about Clinton's key and lasting achievement in the realm of economic growth.

In the years since NAFTA, the Democratic base and

Democratic politicians have become even more violently opposed to free trade. In the summer of 2005, George W. Bush sought passage of the Central American Free Trade Agreement, a far more modest document than NAFTA. *Washington Post* economic reporter Jonathan Weisman described the mood in the House of Representatives thus: "A long, slow erosion of Democratic support for trade legislation in the House is turning into a rout, as Democrats who have never voted against trade deals vow to turn their backs on CAFTA. The sea change [is] driven by redistricting, mounting partisanship and real questions about the results of a decade's worth of trade liberalization."[1]

In 1993, there were 108 House Democrats who voted for NAFTA. In 2005, there were 15—yes, 15—House Democrats voting for CAFTA. As leftist columnist John Nichols put it, "Organized labor is opposed to the Central American Free Trade Agreement. Progressive farm groups are opposed to CAFTA. Environmental groups are opposed to CAFTA. Civil rights groups are opposed to CAFTA. Human rights groups are opposed to CAFTA. Virtually all of the organizations that are associated with what is loosely defined as the Democratic coalition are opposed to the trade deal that Senate Democratic Whip Dick Durbin says 'will hurt American workers, hurt the workers of Central America and create instability in Central America that will force more immigration into the United States.'"[2]

While it is indeed true that many elements of the Democratic base have determined that free trade is responsible for a host of ills—vanishing American jobs, lower-than-desired wages, and so on—no sustained intellectual case remains for erecting trade barriers or imposing protectionist measures. Globalization can be retarded, to some degree, but it cannot be stopped, and the fight against it is a rearguard action that will damage the American economy.

Free trade doesn't only eliminate jobs; it creates new ones. A dynamic economy needs to adapt to new world circumstances. Fighting those circumstances only creates opportunities for other economies to step in and benefit from the new bounties. Many Democrats, particularly those from high-trade states, understand this. While only 7 percent of Democratic House members voted for CAFTA, 23 percent of Democratic senators (10 of 44) did—some of them, like Oregon's Ron Wyden and Washington's Maria Cantwell, otherwise very liberal.

One senator who voted against CAFTA was Hillary Rodham Clinton, and it's clear that vote was nakedly political, cast with an eye toward the "organizations" in the "Democratic coalition" John Nichols mentioned. In earlier years, she had voted to establish free-trade zones with Chile, Singapore, and Vietnam. Those votes were consistent not only with the record of the Clinton administration in which she (sort of) served but also with the interests of the financial markets.

As a senator from New York, the home of Wall Street, Hillary is more than ordinarily sensitive to the words of counsel she receives from financial majordomos like Robert Rubin, her husband's acclaimed treasury secretary and now part of the troika that runs Citigroup, the world's largest financial-services company. Gaining the respect and affection of the financial markets isn't just a senatorial responsibility. It's part of her long-term strategy to secure the Democratic nomination. Remember that she wants to collect so much money so early that she will appear to have a stranglehold on the Democratic nomination a year before the primaries, and to do that she will need executives at firms like Citigroup to work their underlings for "bundled" contributions. (In a bundle, a single person takes the responsibility for contacting, say, 200 other people and getting them to pony up the maximum allowable

$2,000 contribution. Each "bundle," therefore, can total hun-
dreds of thousands of dollars. And at Citigroup, which has
275,000 employees worldwide, there may be 100 people working simultaneously on bundles.)

The vote against CAFTA indicates Hillary felt the need to
tack left on trade in 2005. It's likely big-money Democrats
will not be angry with her for doing so, because it will be
hard to find a Democratic candidate in 2008 who won't
sound like Pat Buchanan when it comes to trade matters.
But that's no reason for Republicans to let Hillary off the
hook. They should highlight her inconsistencies on the matter, and point out, whenever she tries to use the Clinton
administration's economic record to her advantage, that if
she were president, she would almost certainly not support
legislation like NAFTA—and that Democrats in Congress
would use her ascension to the White House to try to retract
elements of currently existing free-trade agreements.

The public likes free trade. Democratic interest groups
don't. There's a canyon there. Toss her into it.

TALK A LOT
ABOUT HEALTH CARE

At the beginning of this book, I said that Hillary's great policy failure during her husband's presidency—the effort to engineer a backdoor government takeover of the American health care system—would not be enough to deny her the presidency. The plan blew up way back in 1994, she'll be running in 2008, and there's obviously a huge gap between Hillary then and Hillary now (a gap that included a Gap dress, but we shouldn't go there, now, should we).

Still, there's an old Jewish joke—a joke about a medicinal cure-all—that might give us some guidance about how to handle the subject of Hillary, her health care fiasco, and the upcoming election. At a funeral, a rabbi is delivering a eulogy when from the back, a woman shouts out, "Hey, Misteh! Give 'im some chick'n soup! Give 'im some chick'n soup!" The rabbi says, "Ma'am, it wouldn't help." To which the lady replies, "It *couldn't hoit!*"

If Republicans decide to place a great deal of emphasis on health care in the next few years in part as a means of reminding people just how close Hillary Clinton came to instituting neo-socialism in the United States, it might not do much good. But it *couldn't hoit*. Because while the ill feelings still lingering from HillaryCare won't in themselves do her in, they can contribute to an overall sense that her judgment is flawed and her policy prescriptions unwise. And at the same time, talking about health care will give the nation the sense that Republicans have something important and valuable to say about one of the most critical matters facing the country.

Hillary sees health care as a touchy subject for her. She did make her first Senate floor speech on the matter, on February 13, 2001, and used the occasion to make rueful note of her past experience with it: "Now, many of my colleagues will remember when I came to Capitol Hill seven years ago with an idea or two about how to improve health care in our country," she said. "We were not successful then. . . . I learned some valuable lessons about the legislative process, the importance of bipartisan cooperation and the wisdom of taking small steps to get a big job done."[1] Interestingly, these words must have been spoken extemporaneously, because they do not appear in the official text of the floor speech that appears on her Senate website.[2] So while she was willing to make reference to her failure on the spur of the moment, she evidently did not want her own official literature to make much of it. And in the subsequent five years, she has delivered just five more speeches dedicated to the subject of health care.

Clearly, then, the Stop Hillary movement can't leave her alone on this matter. If it makes her uncomfortable, her discomfort should only be enhanced. But this can't be done effectively by harking back to 1993 and 1994 and complaining about what she did then. What the Stop Hillary movement can do is highlight the intellectual ferment on the right on the matter of reforming health care, letting a thousand possible reforms bloom. The very fact that there is and will be such activity on the matter will force Hillary to speak about it more frequently. And when she speaks, she herself will be the best and most potent reminder of the disaster she tried to inflict on the country.

I can't think of anything that would make you skip pages more readily than an extensive primer on various health care reform proposals—I skip pages in books like that, and I read them for a living—so let me just mention two of the dozens that have emerged from the febrile precincts of conservative think tanks and innovative political shops.

The most interesting comes from three senior Republican economists—John F. Cogan and Daniel P. Kessler of the Hoover Institution and R. Glenn Hubbard of the Columbia Business School—and can be found in detail in their book *Healthy, Wealthy, and Wise,* published in late 2005.[3] What they explain is that because of longtime quirks in the tax code dating back to World War II, employers who provide health care do not pay taxes on the health care dollars they spend, but individuals who seek their own health care plans have to use their already-taxed income to pay for it. Since people who get insurance from their employer feel (falsely) that they're basically getting something for free, there is an unlimited demand for health care services. But there's no way for anybody to afford to provide unlimited services, and so employers and the organizations that sell them health care have created bureaucratic obstacles to try and keep costs under control. Consumers are dissatisfied and feel mistreated. Meanwhile, freelancers and people who work for small businesses get totally screwed.

So the Cogan-Kessler-Hubbard proposal would provide tax credits for individuals so that they could receive the same level of benefit as someone working for a major employer. This would introduce consumer choice into the system, because someone using his own dollars—even if those dollars are returned to him in the form of later tax-credit money—will always spend less and spend more wisely than someone who thinks he's getting these services for free. There would be far less paperwork, because each individual would effectively be his own gatekeeper, not an HMO. There's a great deal more to the Cogan-Kessler-Hubbard plan, including changes that would level the playing field by no longer allowing Congress to exempt certain employers and providers from state law.

The outgoing Republican governor of Massachusetts, Mitt Romney, has his own innovative health care proposal. On the surface, it would appear similar to Clinton's really rotten original plan because it calls for everyone in the Bay State to be insured. "I don't like calling it universal coverage," Romney told Joe Klein of *Time*, because it "smacks of HillaryCare."[4] Romney wants to use the money Massachusetts pays for the health care of the uninsured poor and combine it with federal health care dollars the state gives Massachusetts by law. That still wouldn't be enough money, so Romney would compel those who are uninsured by choice—mainly younger workers—to join up. He calls it a "personal responsibility system" on the grounds that those who make a conscious decision not to buy health care coverage are betting they won't get hurt—but if they do, they are then simply relying on the generosity of Massachusetts to take care of huge bills they can't possibly afford to pay. Romney's communitarian approach insists that young people take the responsibility of ensuring they do not become wards of the state in this fashion.

Romney's plan is problematic—for one thing, what's to keep those younger workers from simply moving across the border to New Hampshire or Rhode Island so they can save the $2,000 they would have to spend under his system? But the idea of introducing personal responsibility into the system is one very much worth discussing in the context of the 2008 race.

These are substantive plans. There are a dozen others on the right that could become part of the overall discussion. And keeping them very much at the forefront of the national discussion may be a way of keeping Hillary a bit off-balance.

Then there's the possibility that a Republican candidate might decide to make a dramatic maneuver that would delight budget hawks on the right and put Democratic politicians in a hilariously uncomfortable position. The dramatic maneuver would be to call for the abolition of the Medicare prescription drug benefit forced through a reluctant Congress by the Bush administration in late 2003.

Two years after its passage, American seniors were faced with a bewildering array of options from an astounding variety of providers when they were finally forced to choose a plan for themselves. And so a benefit intended to help allay their fears of drug costs run amok was instead breeding confusion and anger about the insanely complicated variety of possible plans. For instance, a health-insurance counselor told the *Pittsburgh Post-Gazette* that Medicare users in his area "are disappointed in this prescription drug benefit because it's very confusing and they don't like the price structuring." The *Post-Gazette* asked the counselor to describe the mood, and he replied, "I'd say there's anger and frustration."[5] Some version of that same story appeared in newspapers across the country, and there's not a younger person in America with a parent above the age of sixty-five who didn't get an earful about the horrors of "Part D."

Now, as far as the nation's health care crisis goes, there are good reasons for a well-considered prescription-drug benefit—primarily, that if people use medications wisely, the amount of money they will need to spend on wildly expensive surgeries and treatments should drop radically and eventually bring down the spiraling cost of Medicare. And politically, the Bush administration had very little choice but to push for its passage—because, as I said earlier, Bush had promised to create the entitlement in 2000 just as the Democrats had and he needed to take the issue off the table in order to win reelection in 2004.

But for many Republicans, particularly budget hawks in Congress, its passage created feelings of extraordinary bitterness. Entitlements like Medicare and Social Security are budgetary time bombs. No matter how much you think they're going to cost, down the road they will invariably be vastly more expensive than you can imagine (even though, as I just said, the theory is that the more money spent on drugs, the less money spent on operations). Republicans who believe in reducing the size of government, not expanding it, were and are appalled by the new entitlement.

They were so upset by it, in fact, that they almost defeated it, in what would have been a political catastrophe for the Bush White House. Only some very questionable strong-arm tactics by the leadership of the House of Representatives ensured its passage. Once a bill is put up for vote in the House of Representatives, members are supposed to vote on the measure within 15 minutes. Using a sneaky maneuver, then–majority leader Tom DeLay managed to keep the clock frozen in place for more than two hours to give him the time he needed to work his will on reluctant House members. They were alternately cajoled and threatened in a variety of ways, and in one case House leaders seemed to have come perilously close to bribery. At the same time, Democrats refused to support the Republican-designed prescription drug benefit. Why? Because it wasn't expensive *enough* for them.

So if the entitlement is unpopular with Republican politicians who want to be fiscally responsible, is unpopular with Democrats because they want to be even more fiscally irresponsible, and is unpopular with the seniors for whom it is supposed to be a lifeline, why keep it? Why not ditch it—and do so at the most politically advantageous time? There is a precedent for such conduct. In 1988, Congress passed and the president signed a "catastrophic health insurance" Medicare package that so angered American seniors that it was voted out of existence the very next year. As health-insurance historian Jonathan Oberlander wrote, "The only substantial expansion in program history was rolled back because of opposition from segments of the elderly population."[6]

Now we've had the second substantial expansion in the history of Medicare, and its reviews are none too good. If the first could be rolled back in 1989, couldn't the second be rolled back in 2008—just in time for a big debate over the matter featuring a very uncomfortable Hillary Rodham Clinton?

It's far too early to say whether this rollback would be a good idea. Republicans will have to wait and see how many seniors choose to opt in to the prescription-drug benefit. Predictions for the first year are that fewer than 20 percent will do so. If that number does not rise in succeeding years, rollback might be just the thing. But if seniors do discover that the program will actually be of modest benefit to them (as it will, if not to the rest of us) and act accordingly, then my putatively brilliant scheme should go into the garbage disposal.

SUGGEST A PULLOUT FROM THE U.N.

Whether Hillary Clinton has become an honest-to-God hawk on military matters or is just playing one on TV—whether, in other words, she has chosen to take a hawkish stance for sheerly political reasons or out of deep post-9/11 conviction—her consistent votes in favor of increased defense spending, homeland security, the Patriot Act, and the wars in Afghanistan and Iraq mean she cannot be dismissed as just another Democrat queasy about military action and American power.

Hillary already has a greater problem with the left wing of her own party than she must have anticipated. Of all the politicians in the United States, no one has a greater vested interest in a favorable outcome in Iraq by 2008 than Hillary Clinton. For, as Mickey Kaus of *Slate* has suggested, that will defang the criticism from the Left and allow her to assume the mantle of statesman—for she will then be shown to have been correct on the matter all along. It is very possible, some would say likely, that by 2008 Americans will think our efforts in Iraq were at least mildly successful and will have a far more positive view of the matter than they did in 2005.

As a result, one classic arrow in the Republican quiver may not be very useful against Hillary—the "soft on defense" arrow. Democrats indicated how intensely they feared the use of this line of attack in 2004 when they nominated a man they believed would be beyond criticism by Republicans because of his own life story and military credentials (oopsie).

If things go badly in Iraq, that won't doom Hillary's candidacy either. Even though memories in America seem to be getting shorter every day, they're not so short that Democrats won't remember what happened the last time they chose a "peace" candidate at a time of war. The situation in Vietnam was horrendous in 1972 when the Democrats nominated George McGovern on a "Come Home, America" platform— and McGovern proceeded to lose in the largest landslide in this country's history. And he didn't lose to a charmer like Ronald Reagan either, but rather to a president who had himself only taken office four years earlier with a mere 43 percent of the vote. That president's name was Richard Nixon, for God's sake. Can you believe Richard Nixon, of all people, could get 61 percent of the electorate to vote for him? Given the tale of 1972, it seems unlikely that the Democrats— despite the power and influence of the Neo-Loony Left—will commit political suicide in 2008 by insisting on a pacifistic McGovernite platform when they have a genuine opportunity to take back the White House.

But there's more to the traditional Republican advantage on matters of foreign policy. While Hillary has earned the right to claim a certain tough-mindedness on these matters, she is part of an overwhelming consensus in the Democratic Party when it comes to discussing America's role in the world. According to that consensus, this nation's safety and security depend on its membership in the "community of nations"—that sweet-sounding euphemism for the groaningly bureaucratic network of international organizations, treaties, and nongovernmental bodies that transcend traditional borders. The most famous of these is, of course, the United Nations, but there are more than a hundred such bodies of which the United States is a member and several others (like the European Union and the European Parliament) in which we have by gift of geography been blessedly spared participation.

In many cases, American participation in the "community of nations" is a benefit to us. It gives us the means to help reformers and liberalizers in other countries to institute the kinds of "transparent" practices that define our political and economic behavior—free and monitored elections, allowing mediating institutions like civic organizations and churches to function as a check on government power, and the introduction of "generally accepted accounting principles." (That may be the most boring term ever devised for one of the most important rules of a free economy—the rule that says the books must be kept in the same way by everybody.) On these matters, Republicans and Democrats can unreservedly agree.

Philosophically, however, there is a world of difference between the parties about America's true place in the community of nations.

For Republicans, there is no question that if there is indeed such a community, the United States is its leader. This is the wealthiest, freest, and most politically stable nation the world has ever seen. It is the most militarily powerful as well. And the United States finds itself in a unique historical position: Since the fall of the Soviet Union, there is no nation challenging America's supremacy.

We Republicans and conservatives have no problem whatsoever with this state of affairs, because we believe America is an unambiguous force for good in the world. And for those who might argue that the unipolar nature of the world is what has made the United States a target of Islamofascists, the response is simple: Osama bin Laden himself said that he believed he could defeat America not because of its strength but because of its weakness. Noting that the United States had pulled Marines from Lebanon in 1983 after a deadly car bombing and pulled Rangers from Somalia after a gang slaughtered eighteen of them, bin Laden declared the United States a "paper tiger."

From that statement by bin Laden and from the baffling behavior of Saddam Hussein—who, it now appears, refused to cooperate with us on the question of the weapons of mass destruction he did not possess because he thought we wouldn't have the guts to go through with our threats to take out his regime—the Right has taken the lesson that American primacy can only be sustained if the world has no doubts that we are strong and determined.

From World War I onward, the United States found itself embroiled in wars with dictators and totalitarians who sought world domination through force of arms and ideological suppression. Inevitably, other powerful adversaries on a par with the Soviet Union, Imperial Japan, and Nazi Germany will rise to challenge us and threaten the world—or so the uninterrupted story of the world tells us. So even as we battle the foe currently threatening us, we must also do what we can to impede the rise of these unknown adversaries.

Thus, the "community of nations" is a useful and valuable thing for the Right so long as it represents a net contribution to these American goals, now and in the future. But for Democrats, liberals, and the Left, the "community of nations" is far more important than that. The "community of nations" is to them an end in itself—in fact, a higher and more important element in guaranteeing world stability, world peace, the advancement of freedom, and meeting the needs of the least fortunate among us than the United States.

The true purpose of the liberal Left's insistence that the United States consider itself no more than a single element in the "community of nations" is that there is a considerable body of opinion on the left that the United States is simply too powerful on its own. Rather like the liberal conviction that wealth should be redistributed simply as a matter of fairness, American liberals in the post–Cold War era seem to believe that America has too much power and that the only way to distribute its power fairly is to have the United States cede some of it to the "community of nations." How does this happen?

Perhaps the best example is the way American environmental organizations and activists—all of them aligned with the Democrats or with the farther-left Greens—want the United States to become a signatory to the Kyoto Protocol governing greenhouse gases. Though Kyoto is usually described as a treaty whose purpose is to reduce global warming, in fact it is far more ambitious and far-reaching than that. It is a blueprint for economic development in the twenty-first century, since it seeks to place regulatory controls on worldwide industrial production for the purpose of saving the environment. And those regulatory controls are designed to level the playing field—to let a nation without much industry build some while highly industrialized countries like the United States are to do less—or pay monetary penalties for failing to live within the bounds of the protocol. In essence, the United States would surrender some of its own industrial production to poorer countries in the developing world.

The United States is not a party to the Kyoto Protocol, though then–vice president Al Gore signed the document in 1997. Before he did so, the Senate passed one of those lovely Sense of the Senate resolutions rejecting its terms by a margin of 95–0, which meant every Democratic senator present voted against it.

And yet Kyoto remains a nearly holy document to the liberal Left. In December 2005, Bill Clinton went to Montreal, where it was being discussed, and insisted that the Bush administration was "dead wrong" to say that Kyoto's terms would be harmful to the U.S. economy. He doesn't believe that, of course, as he proved when he said that if we really put our minds to it here in America, we could make "a serious, disciplined effort to develop energy-saving technology" and meet Kyoto targets.[1] He might as well have said we could invent magical jelly beans that would free us from our dependence on current industrial systems. And were some American company to invent those magical jelly beans, it would doubtless come under pressure from the environmentalists to hand them out for free.

A case even more interesting than the Kyoto Protocol is the United Nations. It is astonishing but true that the U.N. remains a sacrosanct body for the Democratic Party. Making better, more thorough, more constant, and more respectful use of the United Nations is the key to all serious Democratic thinking on foreign policy. The idea is called "multilateralism." But the United Nations of Democratic fantasy bears little relation to the United Nations as it is. When the world is lucky, the United Nations is ineffectual. When the world is less lucky, the United Nations can and often does serve as an active cause of harm. In Africa, U.N. forces sent to keep the peace routinely rape and prostitute the women in the refugee camps they are supposedly protecting. Its Human Rights Commission seats countries like Libya and Syria, where human rights are nonexistent, and Sudan, which literally enslaves Christians.

And then, of course, there is the oil-for-food scandal,

which began as an ostensibly humanitarian way to allow the
people of Saddam's Iraq to get food during the years that nation was under a U.N.-enforced embargo. In short order, oil-
for-food became the largest and most significant financial
scandal in the history of the world, and one in which senior
officials in New York appear to have been directly involved.
We don't yet know the full scope of the scandal, but as much
as $20 billion may have flowed back and forth between Sad-
dam Hussein, cutout companies, and others while starva-
tion and privation continued inside Iraq—and while, back in
New York, the United Nations received a 1 percent transaction commission on every dirty dollar spent.

As the details of the scandal were being uncovered in 2005
(in part by a Senate investigating committee led by Minnesota Republican Norm Coleman), Democrats did rear in
horror—but not at the possibility that the entire United Nations may be a criminal enterprise in the guise of a world
legislative body. Rather, they saved their expressions of
shock and terror for George W. Bush's nominee for the U.S.
ambassadorship at the U.N., John Bolton. Too combative,
they said. Too nasty! And think of it: Bolton once said the
U.N. building could lose ten floors and nobody would miss
them! Democrats actually filibustered Bolton's nomination
and forced Bush to appoint him during a recess (which
means Bolton's term will end at the conclusion of the Congressional term at the end of 2006).

Hillary was one of those filibustering Democrats. Hillary
also has a long record of institutional support for the United
Nations, having made the controversial decision to travel to
Beijing in 1995 as the head of the American delegation for
the U.N.'s Year of the Woman. And her foreign-policy pro-
nouncements are full of invocations of the need for better
cooperation with allies and criticisms of George W. Bush for
his unilateralist approach and his supposed refusal to allow

U.N. weapons inspectors to "finish their work" before the beginning of the war in Iraq—even though it's indisputable that they could have wandered around the country for five years with Saddam still in charge without coming to a conclusion any more definitive than the one they rendered.

Democrats believe deeply in multilateralism. But it presents them with a serious political problem. Compared with a Republican politician who will say he will do whatever it takes to protect and defend the United States no matter what some organizations might have to say about it—and who says he will champion American economic growth and the jobs it creates at home over an international system designed to retard that growth—Democrats sound and look weak. One of the key qualities voters seek in a presidential candidate for whom they can vote is "leadership." It seems intangible, but it really isn't. A candidate will seem like a leader if he embraces America's position as the world's leader and does so unambiguously. If he temporizes or qualifies it, he—or she—just won't seem like as much of a leader.

Republicans have an opportunity to place Democratic multilateralism at the center of the 2008 campaign. They could take stock of the unbelievable scope of the oil-for-food scandal and the corruption it represents and make it a key issue in 2008. They could open a national debate on whether the United States should withdraw from the United Nations in favor of a new organization—an organization made up of the world's democratic nations, all of whom could sit on a Human Rights Commission without causing a worldwide scandal.

A Republican candidate could simply say that the United States might want to revisit the question of the American commitment to the United Nations and whether we and the world have been and can continue to be well served by this sixty-year-old organization that has grown so tarnished by scandal and its own ineffectuality. After all, just because it has existed for sixty years does not necessarily mean it need continue to exist for another sixty—though it certainly can, and though the United States would put no obstacles in the path of its continuation. Should a commission determine that a new organization would be the way to go, the current body would have the right to stay where it is in Manhattan's Turtle Bay, with all the diplomatic and ambassadorial niceties guaranteed under its charter. The United States, however, might choose to move on.

The very suggestion would cause an uproar among liberals and the Left of a sort we haven't seen since Ronald Reagan made a joke about bombing the Soviet Union. Republicans will be denounced as madmen, fanatics courting the hatred of the world, and a million other things. The editorial page of the *New York Times* will shroud itself in black, like the page in Laurence Sterne's *Tristram Shandy* that mourns the passing of Yorick.

All joking aside, the suggestion alone would be greeted as a scandal. It would cause a worldwide panic. It could only be attempted under certain conditions—in particular, even more horrifying revelations in the oil-for-food scandal— otherwise it might make the Republicans who suggested it seem wildly reckless even to those Americans with an un-favorable view of the United Nations.

But think of it, simply, as a political gambit. Would Hillary Clinton be prepared, as part of a presidential race that is bound to be very close, to defend the United Nations hotly? To argue forcefully that the United States cannot do without it? Will those seem like the words of an American leader, or a wussy Democrat?

The virtue of an unambiguous suggestion like this one is that, once again, it makes it impossible for her to sit on the fence and try to find a middle ground—because it takes the middle ground away from her. Even if floating the notion of a U.S. pullout from the U.N. is too risky, Republicans must do all they can to make Hillary's unthinking embrace of multilateralism, and the capitulation it represents to an international community that longs to hold America back a bit, known to the American electorate in 2008.

FIGHT THE CULTURE WAR, BUT WITH DELICACY

There was great shock, and a little bit of awe, in Washington after the 2004 elections when exit polls named "moral values" as the matter of greatest concern to the electorate, followed closely by the economy and then by terrorism. Moral values? The election had revolved almost entirely around the war in Iraq, and yet only 15 percent of voters said that was their primary concern. How did it happen that "moral values" scored so high?

Very quickly, left-wing Democrats and very conservative Republicans came up with the same answer: gay marriage. The election was secretly all about gay marriage. In the spring of 2004, the high court in Massachusetts had declared gay marriage a right under the Fourteenth Amendment to the U.S. Constitution. George W. Bush in turn had thrown his support behind a Constitutional amendment to ban gay marriage. And that was that. Neither Democrats nor Republicans wanted to talk about it very much.

Indeed, the issue was barely discussed during the presidential campaign—with the sole shocking exception of gay-marriage opponent John Kerry pointing out the existence of Dick Cheney's gay daughter in a debate, as if to send a message to socially conservative Democratic voters that these Republican muckety-mucks are just as impure as liberal Democrats. And yet in the weeks following the election, you would have thought it was the hinge on which the election turned—entirely because of those exit polls.

This was perversely pleasing to both camps. For social conservatives, the idea highlighted their power within the Republican camp. For Democrats, there was something comforting in the idea that their defeat came about as a result of reactionary homophobic forces inside America who would never have listened to them anyway.

If you look at it this way, the Republican Party didn't out-argue the Democrats on the pressing matters of national security and the economy. Instead, Bush and Co. won by playing on the supposedly retrogressive and offensive fears of ignorant red-staters. But there is a silver lining, Democrats believe. They like to say that on the matter of social liberalism, America is "evolving," which means that over time, most of the country will come to perceive the anti–gay-marriage position with the same moral outrage with which it now views laws against miscegenation.

But it's absurd to describe gay marriage as the hinge issue of the election. In the first place, if you added the results on terrorism and the war in Iraq together, 34 percent of Americans chose these national-security matters as the key ones in 2004, far outdistancing the 22 percent scored by "moral values." And most important, the term *moral values* wasn't and isn't code for "opposition to gay marriage." If the use of the term *moral values* measured anything other than a platitude—and I'm not sure that it did—it suggested the importance to a large slice of the electorate of what can best be called, simply, tradition.

By tradition, I mean hewing to common standards of personal conduct and comportment that predate the social revolution of the 1960s—living a life within bourgeois family units in which religious observance plays a substantial role. Being married, having kids, and attending church are the three most reliable indicators of whether someone will vote

Republican. This is what Karl Rove understood as he designed the GOP political machine in 2004, which sought to strip-mine the United States for every married churchgoer with children and grandchildren and get every last one of them to vote for Bush. Some—not all, but a great deal—of that 22 percent increase in Bush's vote total from 2000 was due to precisely this tactic.

Bush had particular appeal to such people because his Christian faith plays such a central role in his life. He didn't need to stress his Christian-conservative convictions because they were so intrinsic to him. That made him an easy sell to Rove's new voters. And the fact that those voters turned out in such numbers is good news for Republicans in 2008, because, as noted, the most reliable predictor of whether somebody will vote in the future is whether that person has voted in the past. Having entered the electorate, many of these folk won't leave it.

But there's a caveat: Unless the Republican nominee in 2008 is another professed born-again Christian—which is doubtful—Bush's successor is going to have to work a little harder than he did to generate enthusiasm from the "moral values" voter. And the problem is that those who are not traditionalists themselves are often tone-deaf or worse when it comes to speaking to these matters.

Even though values questions have long tended to favor Republicans when they take center stage, GOP politicians have frequently mishandled them. The worst such case came when Newt Gingrich suggested in 1994 that an appropriate response to the anger over a young mother who murdered her own children was to vote Republican. "How a mother can kill her two children, 14 months and 3 years, in hopes that her boyfriend would like her is just a sign of how sick the system is," he said, "and I think people want to change. The only way you get change is to vote Republican."[1] By the middle of 1995, Gingrich was the most disliked person in America, and that was due in some part to the sensibility that suggested that the political system dominated by Democrats somehow gave Susan Smith leave to drown her own babies.

There can be nothing more delicate than discussions of the private lives and desires of American voters and their relation to the law. But such discussions are now part of the political debate, and though Democrats and liberals are hungry to claim that Republicans put them there, the opposite is true. It wasn't Republicans who put gay marriage on the national agenda but homosexual groups, liberal judges, and the media. Republicans aren't seeking to change the law; they want to *retain* the traditional understanding of it.

On the charged subject of abortion, Republicans and conservatives may stand in opposition to it in all cases, but in terms of the public debate on the matter, they have moved toward a more measured effort—seeking some restrictions rather than spending their energies on an outright ban. That leaves Democrats in the position of arguing the absolute right to an abortion under all circumstances.

———

WHEN IT COMES to these and other charged matters, like the extent of stem-cell and cloning research, what Republicans need as they approach 2008 is to find an appropriate tone to discuss them—to speak far more in sorrow than in anger about maintaining the bourgeois traditions that undergird our freedoms. Let the anger be expressed not by Republicans saddened to be having such fights, but by liberals, leftists, and their allies in the media who will do what they always do in such situations—use name-calling rather than argument with those who disagree with their efforts to expand the definition of marriage and the moral frontiers of science.

In other words, let the antitraditionalists draw first blood. They cannot help themselves—they believe they are in the right and all who oppose them are at best deluded and at worst evil. They are, in other words, mirror images of Newt Gingrich. They will say things and act in a way that will only publicize their views to those who are discomfited by them or who disagree with them. In this regard, the mainstream media's utter disregard for the diversity of opinion on a subject like gay marriage puts blinders on antitraditional activists who can't imagine that anyone on earth might disagree with them (say, because the Bible tells them so). Or they drag out a loudmouth like Pat Robertson to call down Hell's wrath on the unbelievers—when Robertson has long since had his day and the tone of the traditional faithful is now much more clearly represented by a soft-spoken evangelical.

In this way, it will be the liberals themselves who will rally the conservative faithful. It will not be Hillary Clinton, who is far too careful and cautious a politician to place herself on the front lines in the culture war. As we've seen, she has sought to follow her husband's lead and strike a culturally conservative stance on issues like video-game violence and flag-burning—but these are secondary matters. They might sound good to some traditionalists, but when gay marriage is on the table, video-game violence really isn't going to have much of an impact. After all, who *defends* video-game violence?

———

A MORE PRESSING QUESTION is how the Religious Right—which represents a great many but not all of the traditionalists—is going to react in 2008 to a Republican nominee who does not come from their ranks and who may have held positions in the past or even in the present with which they disagree strongly. In this instance, such people will need to think about how valuable it can be to hold someone's political IOU. A victorious Hillary, who won't speak in terms offensive to traditionalists, will nonetheless have handed her IOUs out to liberal groups who will expect her to deliver on their anti-traditionalist wishes once the election is over. Similarly, a GOP candidate who is not part of the Religious Right will have to work hard to establish his bona fides with traditionalists. They will hold his IOUs after the election in terms of staying firm on social issues and appointing cabinet and sub-cabinet members who will not betray their interests.

This is the one case in which the presidency of the first George Bush offers an instructive example. The elder Bush had run his own presidential campaign in 1980 as a liberal Republican with pro-choice sympathies. When he ran in 1988, having now declared himself pro-life, he made it absolutely clear to the leaders of the Religious Right that he was placing himself in their hands and would be in their debt. And indeed he was.

With the exception of his nomination of David Souter to the Supreme Court (who turned out, to Bush's own dismay, to be an Upper West Side liberal in flinty Yankee's clothing), Bush the Elder ran a far more socially conservative White House and administration than Ronald Reagan had. Reagan didn't feel he was in the Religious Right's debt; he felt he had done more for them than they had for him. With the elder Bush, it was the opposite—and whatever reasons there were for his defeat in 1992, he certainly had the enthusiastic support of social conservatives.

Social conservatives should keep this in mind as they ponder the final three points in my ten-point plan.

RUN A REFORM CAMPAIGN

Stopping Hillary isn't just a matter of acquainting the public with her failings. The Republican Party is going to have to show some savage efficiency in dealing with its own failings. The Republican nominee in 2008 has to be an answer, a partial cure, for the diseases afflicting the GOP—just as George W. Bush was in 2000. By running as a compassionate conservative, Bush had acknowledged that the conservatives in Washington who had been running the party deserved some of the criticism they had received for being cold and unfeeling. And by saying that he had "no stake" in the bitter quarrels in Washington in the previous few years, the Texas governor was acknowledging that his own party might have gone too far in pursuing Bill Clinton's impeachment.

The major issue facing the Republican Party in 2008 is corruption—both political and financial. For the purposes of this discussion, let's assume the GOP maintains control of both houses of Congress in 2006 (the likeliest outcome of the next election). If that happens, by 2008 Republicans will have held the House uninterruptedly for fourteen years, controlled the Senate for all but seventeen months of those fourteen years, and been in charge of the White House for the previous eight years. And we've already discussed the negative consequences of this concentration of power when it comes to policy—the explosion in pork-barrel spending, the lack of interest in controlling government spending, the arrogance in seeking to bend or break rules they themselves had designed to prevent corrupt practices. Though the Texas prosecution of leading House Republican Tom DeLay was nothing more than a political vendetta carried out by a rival Democrat, it did shine a harsh light on DeLay's very rough-edged tactics in pursuit of a permanent Republican majority in the House.

But the trouble goes beyond policy corruption into questions of outright bribery and influence peddling. As I write these words, the investigation involving über-lobbyist Jack Abramoff has only just begun bearing fruit—and since it involves at least one key former staffer of DeLay's and at least one Republican congressman, there's a distinct possibility that over the course of the next few years it could take down literally dozens of major figures in the Republican Party, both elected and unelected.

Those involved in the scandal will protest their innocence, which is their right, and will claim that they are being pursued as part of an effort to "get" the Republican Party, which will be partly right, at least as far as the media are concerned. It's true that as a matter of law everyone involved deserves to be considered innocent until proven guilty, but as a matter of politics, every Republican interested in saving America from Hillary had better treat every single person tarnished by the Abramoff scandal as guilty until proven innocent.

The Abramoff scandal is a potential Chernobyl for the GOP, and it has to be contained before it poisons everything. It is an old conservative habit to circle the wagons when the media attack. If that happens this time, the GOP is sunk and Hillary might as well start ordering the new furniture for the Oval Office. The tone that must be struck is one of high dudgeon and disgust.

For 2008, the Republican Party must commit itself to an

agenda of reform. It must accept that things got messy under Republican rule and that the GOP can clean things up. There are measures large and small that both the party and its presidential candidate can discuss and champion. In the 1980s, Congress took aim at cozy White House deals by enacting all sorts of regulations on when and how former executive-branch officials could go to work lobbying their old colleagues and bureaucracies. These rules are pretty strict and have worked pretty well. In the 1990s, Congress also enacted some lobbying reforms on the workings of Capitol Hill, but everybody seems to agree that there are so many holes in them that they're almost useless.

A Republican candidate for president must champion lobbying changes, must speak out against the corruption and guarantee he will do everything in his power to fix it. A chastened Congress will almost certainly go along with him. But it will not be enough to suggest these structural reforms. The next Republican candidate must also take aim at the explosion in earmarks we've talked about—those bits of targeted spending for individual Congressional districts and states. He must promise to do everything in his power to force spending restraint on Congress, including the liberal use of a veto even against bills submitted by his own party. Ordinarily, such a promise and such action would be political suicide for a president with a Congress dominated by members of his own party. But the GOP's corruption problem changes the ordinary dynamic, at least for 2008.

The politician who has been most forthright about his disgust for the growth in earmarks and with the GOP spending spree is John McCain. He has a twenty-three-year record in Washington of fighting against wasteful spending, which is one of the many potential virtues he would bring to a campaign for the presidency. But while he is a reformer of a sort, he's the kind of reformer whose reforms tend to exacerbate the problems they're trying to fix. His campaign-finance-reform measure limited freedom of speech in the name of purifying politics of its reliance on corporate contributions—and then, in the election cycle that followed, billionaires threw more dollars into the presidential race than anyone had ever conceived of before. And there are plenty of reforms he's not too crazy about either—like the effort to reform Senate rules to prevent the promiscuous use of the filibuster against con servative judicial nominees, which he organized a fourteen-senator rump to stymie.

Also, while McCain is a critic of Washington, he is also a creature of Washington. For the purposes of stopping Hillary, the GOP might be wiser to follow its traditional winning playbook and look elsewhere for a presidential candidate.

GO OUTSIDE WASHINGTON FOR A CANDIDATE

The list of possible presidential candidates every election cycle seems to emerge from nowhere and everywhere at the same time, and since it's impossible to tell just where it comes from, wits and wags in Washington refer to its author as a collective—"The Great Mentioner." When a politician's name is on the Great Mentioner's lips, that person will often feel himself propelled into running for president, because, after all, everybody's talking about it.

Because reporters and pundits tend to be concentrated in Washington, and senators are the big stars in Washington (next to the president and vice president), the Great Mentioner is always heard murmuring the names of senators, despite all the evidence that senators tend not to make successful presidential candidates. It rarely mentions a single name out of the 435 members of the House of Representatives, since not a single sitting member of the House has ever been elected president of the United States.* Most individual House members are small fish in a big pond, which isn't a good way to get national attention. And the ones that

---

* You can make a case that James Garfield was, sort of, since he had served in the House for eighteen years until 1880, when he won the presidency—but technically he was a senator at the time because he had been appointed to the Senate from Ohio that same year.

become big fish in that big pond are always compromised in some fashion by the time they become big fish, so they don't seem all that attractive either. Really, the best you can say about senators as presidential candidates is that they're better than House members. Both pale beside governors, who run for president far less frequently but have a much better winning percentage. Since 1960, only 24 percent of major candidates have been governors, while 36 percent have been senators.[1] Yet only one sitting senator made it to the White House, while four sitting or former governors have.

Governors get things done—as opposed to legislators, who, in Sherman Edwards's brilliantly sarcastic lyric from the Broadway musical *1776*, "piddle, twiddle, and resolve / Not one damn thing do we solve." In general, the Senate represents everything about Washington that ordinary people dislike. If there's one prevailing rule of contemporary politics, it's that Republicans succeed when they look outside Washington for a candidate and suffer when they stick with a Beltway guy. A non-Washington Republican can always speak to the dissatisfaction and disgust many GOP voters feel for the federal government and its heavy hand—and can claim that, as a politician from outside Washington forced to abide by the bullying rules laid down by Congress, he knows more about the way Washington is mismanaged than anyone. That message goes down best of all in the primaries with committed conservative voters, and the non-Washington candidates usually have a field day in debates by pointing out the ways in which the Washington guys have screwed the little guy.

Even so, when it comes to 2008, the Great Mentioner keeps on mentioning one Washington insider—and in the case of John McCain, it's not only mentioning, it's yodeling, it's screaming, it's shouting his name from the rooftops. Never mind all of the potential shortcomings and pitfalls that might arise from his candidacy, as discussed. The Great Mentioner has never loved a Republican the way it loves John McCain. If McCain chooses not to run, the Great Mentioner might just commit Great Suicide.

But there are other names, many other names, of potential presidential candidates. These are the Republican governors—twenty-eight of them. And yet their names are largely unknown to even the most avid news-follower, because the Great Mentioner simply doesn't *do* the flyover states. Tim Pawlenty of Minnesota is one—a pro-life reformist with a notably successful record of conservative governance in a state that goes Democratic in presidential races. Those ten electoral votes from Minnesota could come in handy in a close race. Ever heard of him?

There's Mark Sanford, the governor of South Carolina, who was the leading budget-cutter in the House of Representatives during his three terms from 1995 to 2001—a tenure he ended because he actually lived up to his campaign promise to limit his own time in the House to three terms. He says he's not running for president, but South Carolina is an early primary state and he could presumably win its delegates easily. But could you pick Mark Sanford out of a lineup?

Oh, the Great Mentioner isn't entirely silent when it comes to governors. For instance, it speaks of one in particular. His name is George Pataki. He is the governor of New York. And that's why the Great Mentioner knows who he is and is intrigued by him—because New York is just one air shuttle stop away. George Pataki is also the person primarily responsible for the rebuilding effort at Ground Zero—where, as of this writing, more than four years after the attacks, not a single ounce of concrete has been poured. Pataki's calamitous mishandling of Ground Zero made it impossible for him to run again for governor, and should he enter the Republican primaries in 2008, the first debate would feature just about every other candidate bringing up his dereliction and ensuring that the only people who might actually vote for him would be relatives—and close relatives at that.

Because Massachusetts is one shuttle stop away from New York, the Great Mentioner also occasionally murmurs the name of Governor Mitt Romney. Romney, an accomplished businessman and genuinely creative politician, might be the central-casting choice for the Republican nomination but for one inconvenient but unmistakable fact: He is a member of the Church of Jesus Christ of Latter-Day Saints. As a member of a minority religion, Romney is almost certainly unelectable in the United States in 2008. This is something the Great Mentioner finds it rude to say, and speaking as a Jew myself, I wish it were not so. But it is so, and a serious political analysis must deal with the world as it is rather than the world as one might wish it to be.

A bid by Romney for the nomination will cause newspapers and television channels to write articles about the Mormon church and its tenets—and the fact that it considers itself the true version of Christianity rather than one of the branches of Christianity will be very disturbing to base Republican voters, most of whom will be learning about it for the first time. Granted, no religion and its founding miracles sound sane when described from the outside, but still, tell that to people who find out that Mormons baptize the dead in absentia, that a truly pious man can become a god himself after death, and that God's heavenly city on earth will be built in and around Independence, Missouri.

The United States is 74.5 percent Christian and less than 1 percent Mormon. In a 2002 survey done by Pew, 87 percent of Americans said religion played a very important or somewhat important part in their lives.[2] American voters want to feel some bond of commonality with their president. Romney's LDS beliefs will be alienating. Romney is not the man to defeat Hillary.

The notion that Republicans do best when they look outside Washington has given rise to some interesting but ultimately foolish ideas about unconventional choices for the GOP. For example, Dick Morris wrote an entire book arguing that the only person who could beat Hillary Clinton is Secretary of State Condoleezza Rice. I am second to no one in my admiration of Condi Rice, but if there is a single sentence in this book that you should commit to memory, it is this:

The presidency is not an entry-level job.

It's preposterous to assume that anyone in the modern era will make his or her political debut as an elected official by winning the White House on the first go-round. Only three times in our history have we elected nonpoliticians president. Ulysses S. Grant won the Civil War prior to his run. Dwight D. Eisenhower won World War II prior to his. The next time somebody is directly responsible for saving the last best hope of earth or all of Western civilization, he or she can have the presidency with my blessing, and the country's. (The third was Herbert Hoover. Anybody want to use him as a model?) Until then, the public will want—and the demands of running for office will necessitate—a candidate who, like good steel, has been tempered and sharpened by experience, who can remain calm under fire, and who knows when to give as good as he's getting.

In my view, the best person to take on Hillary Clinton and defeat her has been neither senator, congressman, nor governor. Nor does he fit a politically correct conservative checklist. But he's the most interesting and exciting figure in Republican politics, precisely the kind of star the GOP will need.

NOMINATE RUDY

It's an amazing thing. Rudolph Giuliani has not served in public office since January 2002. The office he held, the mayoralty of New York City, is known as a graveyard for those ambitious to use it as a steppingstone to other political jobs. And yet in every poll of Republican primary voters about whom they would prefer to be the nominee in 2008, Giuliani comes out first or second, neck and neck with John McCain and nobody else even choking on their dust. In a December 2005 poll taken by RT Strategies, Giuliani and McCain tied with 25 percent (without McCain in the race, Giuliani received 33 percent). A month earlier, Giuliani led McCain 34–31 in a *Wall Street Journal* poll.

Why is this so striking? Simply this: While McCain was constantly in the media in 2005, being interviewed on television chat shows and appearing in news stories on subjects as various as torture, cable-television prices, and steroids in baseball, Giuliani was all but invisible. He could have been on television seven nights a week but chose not to do so. Practically the only time he appeared in public was in advertising or in campaign appearances supporting candidates for public office—his successor Mike Bloomberg in New York, failed gubernatorial candidate Doug Forrester in New Jersey.

According to *Forbes* magazine, in 2005 Giuliani ranked eightieth among the nation's celebrities—not its politicians, but *celebrities*, as one of the nation's three most hotly sought-after public speakers. *Forbes* counted it up: In 2005, Giuliani was the subject of 620,000 Web searches, was mentioned in 7,815 news articles, and was discussed on nearly 1,300 television programs.[1] There were only two other people on the list not in show business or sports in the top 100. One was Jack Welch, former chairman of General Electric, who came in at #83. The other was Bill Clinton, who came in at #56.

What this tells us is just how formidable a public figure Rudy Giuliani really is, even now. The events of September 11 are nearly five years in the past, and yet Giuliani remains the only American figure whose enhanced standing as a result of the attacks on America remains undiminished. The enthusiasm he provoked because of his stalwart, calm, restrained but emotional response to the destruction of the Twin Towers and the massive loss of life there has endured because the response was genuine and because the enthusiasm was entirely deserved.

For what Rudy Giuliani did in the immediate aftermath of the attack on New York was not all that different from what he did in the midst of any crisis during his mayoralty. In each case—a terrible fire, a water-main break, the crash of TWA Flight 800, a neighborhood blackout—he donned the garb of an emergency worker, toured the scene, gathered the heads of his agencies, designed a plan of action, and then made public appearances during which he informed the city in exhaustive detail about what was going on.

Himself trapped in a building near the World Trade Center, Giuliani had to keep his head about him in order to find his way to safety, helping others along the way. He had to collect himself to do his job, only to learn that three of the four most senior members of the city's fire department had been killed—heartbreaking news that would soon be followed by word that they had been joined in certain death by another 300 firefighters and scores of police officers as well.

And yet there he was, only hours later, standing before cameras and offering a kind of strong reassurance the country had yet to receive from any public official. "We will strive now to save as many people as possible and to send a message that the city of New York and the United States of America is much stronger than any group of barbaric terrorists," he said. "I want the people of New York to be an example to the rest of the country and the rest of the world that terrorism can't stop us."

God knows it could have been otherwise. During major disruptions at other times in the city's recent history, looting had been commonplace. This time there was none. It is possible to ascribe the social peace to the wonderful élan shown by New Yorkers after the attacks, but something far more important was at work: New York's reaction was in part the result of changes in the city's fabric wrought by Giuliani's own revolutionary and extraordinary mayoralty.

He was elected in 1993 to bring order to a city on the verge of civil collapse. And he did so in a manner suggestive of the kinds of policies and approaches he would campaign on were he to run for president and that he would attempt to institute should he make it to the White House. He enlarged the size of the police department and supervised a wholesale redesign of its methods to make it more effective—with the astounding result that crime in New York City during his mayoralty declined by 57 percent.

Those who wish to pooh-pooh this achievement say that because crime dropped elsewhere in America at the same time, New York was simply part of a larger social trend. But in fact, more than half of the national decline in crime was solely attributable to the drop in Giuliani's New York, which houses about 2.5 percent of the population of the United States. There was no "trend." Giuliani and his police department—and their revolutionary policies, which spread like wildfire—*were* the trend.

Of course, in a country where crime is at an all-time low, a politician's decade-old record against it won't mean very much. The point here is that Giuliani proved himself the rarest of creatures: a politician who combined a deeply conservative approach (law and order) with an innovative streak and an astounding degree of the necessary leadership quality Alexander Hamilton called "energy in the executive."

The crime stuff is well known. What is less well known, and will come as a pleasant surprise to Republican primary voters, is the degree to which Giuliani's mayoralty was locked in a constant and startlingly successful battle against the shibboleths of present-day liberalism.

Ever since the 1960s, New York has been governed by a weird and immensely powerful public-private partnership. The outrageously corrupt public-sector unions worked in lockstep with city agencies and the City Council to expand benefits while simultaneously diminishing union responsibility. Activists have colluded with judges to force city agencies into consent decrees that require the agencies to give taxpayer money to the activists, who then live parasitically off the agencies they are supposed to monitor.

Giuliani would have none of it. He fought and fought and fought with unmistakable, and to his enemies often lunatic, passion—trying to sell off unnecessary city hospitals, laying off thousands of city workers in the teeth of concerted opposition, refusing to sign new consent decrees and fighting old ones in court, and insisting on accountability throughout the city bureaucracy.

When he became mayor, new rules had just gone into effect granting his office far greater authority over the city budget than it had ever had before—and he used it. He used a power called "rescission" and refused to spend money on wasteful matters appropriated by the overwhelmingly Democratic and liberal City Council. Though forced by law to balance the city budget, he pushed through $2.5 billion in tax cuts and sought far more. He forced the elimination of several insanely antibusiness taxes (like one on hotel rooms that had cost New York hundreds of millions in precious convention business before the crime turnaround made the city a desirable place again).

But his war on liberalism was not merely budgetary. Take education. He undertook a seven-year fight to wrest control of the city's disastrous elementary schools from a corrupt system of neighborhood school boards, an effort that ultimately came to fruition after he left office. He strongly urged the privatization of failing schools, the institution of school choice throughout the city system, and the creation of charter schools. He stood almost alone among urban leaders in suggesting that bilingual education was a disaster for those living in Spanish-speaking households.

He ended the disastrous policy of "open admissions" at the city's colleges, which had once been a glorious example of public education and had since become a nightmarish example of intellectual rot. By instituting standardized testing, Giuliani has made the city's colleges a path for achievement instead of a warehouse of failure.

He instituted the most far-reaching urban effort in support of the national welfare-reform bill, and by the time he left office an astounding 640,000 New Yorkers were no longer on the dole.

And then there was his surprising social conservatism. It took twenty-one favorable rulings by judges before his enemies threw in the towel and stopped battling a policy he had designed to get rid of pornography distributors in family neighborhoods. Most notoriously, he went to war with the Brooklyn Museum, which staged an exhibition of "transgressive" art featuring a Virgin Mary covered in feces. Giuliani declared the exhibit "anti-Catholic," which it certainly was. He discovered that the museum actually leased the land on which it sat from the city. Using his budgetary authority, he withheld some of the grant money the city paid to the museum and then took it to court seeking its eviction and the firing of its board of directors.

It would be impossible to overestimate the rage this audacious move induced in the city's left-liberal community, which had already decided (in its usually charming fashion) that Giuliani was a new Hitler because he defended his cops against false charges of racist murder instead of throwing them to the dogs of liberal society.

This may all be old news, but what it should prove to GOP primary voters is that the Rudy of 9/11 is made of hard stuff in all sorts of ways. He doesn't care what the *New York Times* says about him; in fact, he uses the *New York Times* as a negative bellwether. In his eight years as mayor, he instituted conservative governance of a sort that America had never seen before. And it wasn't on that small a scale either. For while he was "only" mayor of a city, if that city were a state, its 8 million people would make it the eleventh-largest in the union.

The question is whether this beloved, popular, and profoundly conservative figure can overcome the two major obstacles in the path to the nomination. They are his statements in favor of abortion rights and his support for homosexual civil unions.

In 1999, he told CNN, "I'm pro-abortion. I'm pro gay rights." Ten years earlier, during his first unsuccessful run for City Hall, Giuliani told the talk-show host Phil Donahue that though he had deep reservations about abortion, he supported the use of public money to pay for the procedure. "I do that in spite of my own personal reservations," he said in 1989. "I have a daughter now; if a close relative or a daughter were pregnant, I would give my personal advice, my religious and moral views . . . which would be that I would help her with taking care of the baby." But if the woman chose to have an abortion, "I'd support that. I'd give my daughter the money for it."² In 1999, he said he opposed a ban on the barbaric practice of partial-birth abortion, a ban that has since become the law of the land.

These remarks will no doubt be deeply disturbing to the party's socially conservative wing. What Giuliani was implicitly criticizing in 1989 was the Hyde Amendment, which barred the use of federal funds for abortions—as sacrosanct a piece of socially conservative legislation as exists. As for gay rights, Giuliani did sign a domestic-partnership law in New York City, the precursor to the kinds of "civil unions" now being performed elsewhere in the country.

What can Giuliani do about these off-the-reservation statements? He has two choices. He can defend them, say these are his personal views, that he respects the views of others but there it is, there you have it, and there it stands. Or . . . he can change them, to some degree.

Let me explain what I mean by this. When Giuliani said what he said in 1989, he was running for mayor of New York. No one running for mayor of New York could win as mayor of New York without being a supporter of abortion rights then or now. When he said what he said about abortion and gay rights in 1999, he was under intense pressure to run against Hillary Clinton in her New York Senate race. He would have had no chance to defeat her in the Senate race if he espoused pro-life views, and certainly support for gay rights would have been an absolute necessity. The conservative Giuliani could never have been elected mayor—and could not have won the Senate race from which he suddenly removed himself in 2000 when he discovered he had prostate cancer and had decided to leave his wife—without paying some minor obeisance to social-liberal orthodoxy.

What Giuliani could say now is this: You know what? In my heart, I have always been pro-life, but in order to serve the people as a public official, I could not speak from the heart about this one issue. And as the years have passed and technology has revealed more and more to us about the unborn, I feel that moral caution requires us to give greater credence to the view that the unborn fetus is a living being than the view that says it is disposable.

As for civil unions, he can simply say that he supports what Vice President Dick Cheney has supported—that he believes marriage is between a man and a woman and he will fight to keep that definition unchanged, but that if states and localities wish to recognize civil unions as valid contracts, he has no problem with that.

Okay, so since we're talking turkey here and being ruthlessly honest, the question now is: Can he get away with this? History indicates that he can, if he remains committed to pro-life policies from here on out.

It has been the unstated policy of the pro-life movement that every politician gets a chance to change his mind on the matter and earn the movement's support. Ronald Reagan signed the most liberal abortion law ever passed when he was governor of California, but later declared himself pro-life and was lionized by the movement for it. George Bush the Elder ran for president in 1980 as a frankly pro-choice candidate fighting against those lunatic pro-lifers. By 1988, he had changed his mind, and that was fine with them. In 1996, everybody in the pro-life movement assumed Bob Dole was really pro-choice, but he had voted pro-life throughout his Senate career and so he passed muster. In 1996, Steve Forbes ran for president as a pro-choice Republican—and then, when he lost the nomination, refashioned himself a pro-lifer and sought (with some success in 1999) to challenge the ever-pro-life George W. Bush for the social-conservative vote.

They did it, and Rudy can do it too. He would get blasted for it by the liberal media, which would call him a flip-flopper and a sellout to the Religious Right. And given the deep antagonism toward the mainstream media that resides within Rudy Giuliani's bosom, his passion for his newfound position would only grow over time.

The only other question this raises is whether if he made so public a change of position, his reputation for integrity would be damaged. The answer is, probably, yes, a little bit. But you can't have it all. And if Rudy Giuliani wants to win the presidency, which will require the enthusiasm of that social-conservative vote Karl Rove captured in 2004, he will have to stand up and declare himself opposed to abortion. Or he will not win—and Hillary will.

If there's one thing that Rudy Giuliani's political career demonstrates, it's that he's willing to commit to a controversial course for a higher purpose. Changing his stance on abortion would be controversial. Defeating Hillary Clinton while becoming president himself—could there be any higher purpose?

Conclusion

THE BATTLE OVER IDEAS

A work of political prognostication like this one is bound to get some things wrong. We can't know what will happen tomorrow, let alone two years from now. If this decade has taught us anything, it is that that the unhappily unexpected event can change the country and the world in an instant, and alter the political landscape as well.

Maybe Rudy Giuliani will decide to take a starring role on *Law & Order* instead of seeking the presidency. Maybe John McCain will decide to skip the rigors of the road and sit at home with Chris Matthews massaging his feet every hour on the hour. Maybe Mitt Romney will prove me wrong and by 2009 he will be the first self-described saint ever elected to the highest office in the land. (Oh, sorry—I forgot about Jimmy Carter.) We only speculate on what will happen between these people and the nation they might lead, or what events may occur that might spin the next election on an unforeseeable axis.

And maybe Hillary Clinton won't be the Democratic nominee after all.

What we *do* know is that the great ideological divide will remain—the divide between liberals and conservatives, between traditionalists and moral experimenters, between tax-cutters and tax-raisers, between American nationalists and American multilateralists, between those who want to limit government and those who want to expand it, between those who believe the War on Terror can be won and those who aren't really sure it exists.

This is the fight that matters. This is the fight Republicans must wage. Smart Democrats like Hillary Clinton will try to deemphasize ideology and stress instead that Republicans have been in power too long, have grown too corrupt, and have managed the country incompetently. If they succeed in their task, then 2008 will be their year, for all the reasons outlined within these pages. Democrats were faced with a seemingly insuperable challenge to their world view and their relevance by the success of Congressional Republicans and, especially, the transformative presidency of George W. Bush. They did not go gentle into that political night. Democrats have, instead, rallied and regrouped. They are flush with money and fueled by passion. And they have one of the most famous people in the world to lead their effort to take back Washington and the nation—a sophisticated political animal uniquely positioned to become the first woman president of the United States. She is widely disliked, it is true, but in the polarized climate dominating the first decade of the twenty-first century, all political stars become intensely controversial sooner or later.

In every way, the time would seem ripe for a national partisan flip in the direction of the Democrats and Hillary Clinton—every way but one. And it happens to be the most important one. When it comes to ideas about how to protect Americans, ensure prosperity, expand opportunity, limit the scope of government, and spread the democratic gospel throughout the world, Democrats and liberals have little of value to contribute. They exist primarily to stand athwart Republicans and conservatives in a desperate partisan effort to delay or block the implementation of innovative and creative ideas whose purpose is to make America better and safer, and the world freer.

So if Republicans can stay focused on the battle over ideas—the battle in which they have the upper hand—and do so by nominating a candidate who can explain, defend, and advance those ideas while keeping his party united, then they will prevail and stop Hillary Clinton or whomever the Democrats see fit to nominate.

Okay. I've done my bit. Now get to work.

NOTES

INTRODUCTION: AN OPEN LETTER TO CONSERVATIVES AND REPUBLICANS

1. "Clinton: Hillary Would Be Better President," Associated Press, November 4, 2005.

2. Mark Blumenthal, "Hillary, the Blogs and the Base," Mystery pollster.com, January 6, 2006.

CHAPTER 1: YES, SHE HAS "HIGH NEGATIVES"—AND THEY MIGHT EVEN HELP HER

1. "Party Affiliation and Political Philosophy Show Little Change, According to National Harris Poll," The Harris Poll #19, Harrisinteractive.com, March 9, 2005.

2. Harris Poll #19.

3. The entire text of Hillary Rodham's commencement address can be found at a website called "Gifts of Speech," at http://gos.sbc.edu/r/rodham.html.

4. Quoted in Joyce Milton, *The First Partner: Hillary Rodham Clinton* (New York: William Morrow, 1999), pp. 59–60.

5. Michael Weisskopf, "Energized by Pulpit or Passion, the Public Is Calling," *Washington Post*, February 1, 1993.

6. "Guns in America: National Survey on Private Ownership and Use of Firearms," National Institute of Justice, May 1997.

7. Dan Balz, "Clinton Concedes Marital Wrongdoing," *Washington Post*, January 27, 1992.

CHAPTER 2: AS THINGS STAND, SHE'S NOT TOO LIBERAL TO BE ELECTED

1. The specific votes the American Conservative Union used for its rating can be found at http://www.acuratings.org/singlerecord.asp?RepID=404&RatingsYear=2004.

2. Russell Kirk, *The Conservative Mind* (Chicago: Regnery Gateway, 1953).

3. Final 2000 vote totals can be found at http://www.fec.gov/pubrec/fe2000/prespop.htm.

4. Final 2004 vote totals can be found at http://www.cnn.com/ELECTION/2004/pages/results/.

5. George W. Bush, "The Future of Educational Reform," speech delivered at the Manhattan Institute, available at http://www.manhattan-institute.org/html/bush_speech.htm.

CHAPTER 3: IF A WOMAN CAN BE ELECTED PRESIDENT—AND A WOMAN CAN—HILLARY CAN

1. The data can be found at http://www.maristpoll.marist.edu/usapolls/PZ051021.htm.

2. Rebecca Traister, "Thelma for President," *Salon*, September 29, 2005.

3. "Hillary Rodham Clinton as Feminist Heroine," roundtable discussion, *The American Enterprise Magazine*, July/August 2000.

CHAPTER 4: SO SHE'S NOT WELL LIKED. SO WHAT?

1. Dan Balz, Shailagh Murray, and Peter Slevin, "Voter Anger Might Mean an Electoral Shift in '06," *Washington Post*, November 6, 2005.

2. Tod Lindberg, "An Electoral Shift in 2006?," *Washington Times*, November 8, 2005.

CHAPTER 6: THE ANNUS HORRIBILIS

1. "Pork: A Microcosm of the Overspending Problem," Cato Institute, available at http://www.cato.org/pubs/tbb/tbb-0508-24.pdf.

CHAPTER 7: THE GRASSROOTS GROWL AND THE SIREN SONG OF SCHISM

1. Quoted in Michael Janofsky, "In California, Border Is Focus of an Election," *New York Times*, December 4, 2005.

2. "Congratulatons to John Campbell," HughHewitt.com, December 7, 2005.

3. Pete Winn, "Dobson: Compromise on Nominees a Complete Betrayal," CitizenLink, www.family.org, May 24, 2005.

4. Matt Bai, "Fight Club," *New York Times Magazine*, August 10, 2003.

5. The full text of McCain's February 28, 2000, remarks can be found at http://www.everything2.com/index.pl?node_id=489542.

CHAPTER 8: THE NOT-REPUBLICAN PARTY AND THE NEO-LOONY LEFT

1. Richard Benedetto, "Bush Approval Hits 39%," *USA Today*, October 17, 2005.

2. The most comprehensive poll records over time are kept by John McIntyre and Tim Bevan at their website, RealClearPolitics.com.

3. The Harris Poll's 2005 data can be found at http://harrisinteractive.com/harris_poll/index.asp?PollYear=2005.

4. York breaks down the donations to the Democratic-supporting 527 groups America Coming Together and the Media Fund: "[Hedge fund billionaire George] Soros alone had given $20 million. . . . And the list of contributors grew longer and longer. . . . There was Hollywood producer Stephen Bing, who gave $12 million. There was Hyatt hotel heiress Linda Pritzker, whose family gave $5 million. And the Service Employees International Union, which gave $3 million. And Massachusetts technology entrepreneur Terry Ragon, who gave $3 million. And Texas technology executives Jonathan McHale and Christine Mattson, who together gave $3 million. And the American Federation of State, County, and Municipal Employees, which gave $2.1 million. And New York philanthropist Lewis Cullman, who gave $2 million. And Rockefeller heir Alida Messinger, who gave $1.5 million. And Agnes Varis, head of AgVar Chemicals, who gave $1.5 million. And Illinois broadcasting magnate Fred Eychaner, who gave $1.5 million. And Seattle tech entrepreneur Robert Glaser, who gave $1.2 million. And the Teamsters Union, which gave $1 million. And Colorado entrepreneur Tim Gill, who gave $1 million. And television producer Marcy Carsey, who gave $1 million. And Pennsylvania financier Theodore Aronson, who gave $1 million. And Oregon publisher Win McCormack, who gave $1 million. And heiress Anne Getty Earhart, who gave $1 million. And Texas technology entrepreneur James H. Clark, who gave $1 million. And the American Federation of Teachers, which gave $1 million. And Florida millionaire Dan Lewis, who gave $1 million. And Ohio philanthropist Richard Rosenthal, who gave $1 million. And clothing entrepreneur Susie Tompkins Buell, who gave $1 million. And those were just the ones who contributed $1 million or more." See Byron York, *The Vast Left Wing Conspiracy* (New York: Crown Forum, 2005), pp. 87–88.

5. Chris Cillizza and Peter Slevin, "Sympathetic Vibrations," *Washington Post*, November 27, 2005.

6. For the details of the Ney-Kidan-Boulis affair, I owe an enormous debt to the brilliant Matthew Continetti and his account of the matter, "Money, Mobsters, Murder," in the November 28, 2005, issue of the *Weekly Standard*.

7. "Loser of the Year, Part III" can be found at http://coldhearted truth.com/index.php?m=20050102.

8. "Soros Says Kerry's Failings Undermined Campaign Against Bush," Bloomberg.com, January 30, 2005.

9. Matt Bai, "Machine Dreams," *New York Times Magazine*, August 21, 2005.

10. David Henson, "Bush, Sheehans Share Moments," *The Reporter* (Vacaville, Calif.), June 24, 2004.

11. Cindy Sheehan, "Thinking About Hillary," LewRockwell.com, October 24, 2005.

12. "Clinton Says Iraq Invasion Was a Big Mistake," Associated Press, November 16, 2005.

13.   Jim Fitzgerald, "Clinton: Immediate Exit a Mistake," Associated Press, November 21, 2005.

14.   Cynicor, "Hillary, You Have Two Weeks," DailyKos.com, November 17, 2005.

15.   Dan Balz, "Sen. Clinton Calls for Party Truce, United Front," *Washington Post*, July 26, 2005.

16.   Kos, "H. Clinton and the DLC," DailyKos.com, July 26, 2005.

17.   The text of the letter can be found at http://www.clinton.senate.gov/issues/nationalsecurity/index.cfm?topic=iraqletter.

18.   Steve Gettinger, "Will the House Dance to Dole's Tune?," *Congressional Quarterly*, April 3, 1996.

19.   Dick Morris and Eileen McGann, *Condi vs. Hillary* (New York: Regan-Books, 2005), p. 273.

POINT #1: SMOKE HER OUT

1.   "Hillary Clinton Targets New Rise in Video Game Violence," Agence France-Presse, November 29, 2005.

2.   The text of this speech can be found at http://clinton.senate.gov/~clinton/speeches/2005125A05.html.

3.   Quoted in Farhad Manjoo, "Should We Stay or Should We Go?," *Salon*, December 9, 2005.

POINT #2: MAKE HER VOTE

1.   In 2003, 459 votes were cast; in 2004, an election year, 216 were cast; in 2005, the number was 450.

2.   Evan Thomas, "Trench Warfare," *Newsweek*, November 15, 2004.

3.   Jim Drinkard, "Rove Speaks Out on Bush Win," *USA Today*, November 8, 2004.

4.   Peter Khiss, "Buckley and Moynihan in Final Debate," *New York Times*, November 1, 1976.

5.   Paul Farhi and Helen Dewar, "Kerry Drops Campaign Trip for Senate Vote That Wasn't," *Washington Post*, June 23, 2004.

6.   "Senate Rejects Extension on Unemployment Benefits," Associated Press, May 11, 2004.

7.   Farhi and Dewar.

8.   Results of the Battleground Poll are available at www.tarrance.com/battleground.html.

9.   Bob Somerby, "Spinning Kerry," DailyHowler.com, July 29, 2004.

POINT #3: MAKE HER CRITICIZE TAX CUTS

1.   The chart can be found at http://www.treas.gov/press/releases/reports/revenue%20growth.jpg.

2.   *Today* show, September 7, 2005.

3.   "Hillary Clinton Emerging as High-Profile Critic of Administration's Katrina Effort," *White House Bulletin*, September 7, 2005.

4. Beth Fouhy, "San Francisco Rolls Out the Red Carpet for the Clintons," Associated Press, June 28, 2004.

POINT #4: TALK UP FREE TRADE
1. Jonathan Weisman, "CAFTA Reflects Democrats' Shift from Trade Bills," *Washington Post,* July 6, 2005.
2. "John Nichols, "Democrats Blew It on CAFTA Vote," *Capital Times,* July 5, 2005.

POINT #5: TALK A LOT ABOUT HEALTH CARE
1. Raymond Hernandez, "Health Care Is Mrs. Clinton's First Item on Senate Floor," *New York Times,* February 14, 2001.
2. That official text can be found at http://clinton.senate.gov/news/statements/details.cfm?id=233837&&.
3. *Healthy, Wealthy, and Wise: Five Steps to a Better Health Care System* (Washington: AEI Press, 2005). Hubbard was chairman of the Council of Economic Advisers under the current President Bush; Cogan was deputy director of the Office of Management and Budget under Presidents Reagan and Bush the Elder; Kessler is a professor at Stanford Business School, but he'll have some fancy Washington title someday too, no doubt.
4. Joe Klein, "The Republican Who Thinks Big on Health Care," Time.com, December 4, 2005.
5. Joe Fahy, "Confusion, Frustration Abound As Drug Program Gets Under Way," *Pittsburgh Post-Gazette,* November 6, 2005.
6. Jonathan Oberlander, *The Political Life of Medicare* (Chicago: University of Chicago Press, 2003), p. 211.

POINT #6: SUGGEST A PULLOUT FROM THE U.N.
1. Charles J. Hanley, "Bush 'Flat Wrong' on Kyoto, Clinton Tells Global Audience," *Globe and Mail* (Toronto), December 9, 2005.

POINT #7: FIGHT THE CULTURE WAR, BUT WITH DELICACY
1. Thomas B. Rosenstiel and Edith Stanley, "Gingrich Tames Rhetoric, Savors 'Speaker,'" *Los Angeles Times,* November 9, 1994.

POINT #9: GO OUTSIDE WASHINGTON FOR A CANDIDATE
1. Barry C. Burden, "United States Senators as Presidential Candidates," *Political Science Quarterly,* 2002.
2. "Americans Struggle with Religion's Role at Home and Abroad," Pew Research Center for People and the Press, March 2002.

POINT #10: NOMINATE RUDY
1. "The Forbes Celebrity 100," Forbes.com, December 2005.
2. Quoted in "Giuliani Clarifies Abortion Remarks," Newsmax.com, March 18, 2005.

ACKNOWLEDGMENTS

For giving me a home away from home to finish this book, I am, as ever, profoundly grateful to the Hoover Institution and its director, John Raisian—and John's associates David Brady and Mandy MacCalla. For companionship at Hoover, you can't beat the most vivid man I've ever known, Arnold Beichman, or my old buddy Peter Robinson.

As far as collegiality goes, my *New York Post* colleagues and friends Bob McManus, Mark Cunningham, and Col Allan set the standard. My debt to Rupert Murdoch, as I've said before, is inexpressible.

For writerly sympathy, I must thank my father, Norman.

For Machiavellian counsel, I owe a conspiratorial debt to Lucianne Goldberg.

For their comments and criticisms of the manuscript, I am grateful to Tod Lindberg, Daniel Casse, and my mother, Midge Decter Podhoretz.

For her advocacy, a shout-out to Joni Evans.

For research assistance, a wave to Heather Smith.

For careful and literate editing, hearty handshakes to Jed Donahue of Crown Forum, and Toni Rachiele.

For giving my life transcendent meaning, my daughter, Shayna.

For everything, Ayala.

INDEX

ABOUT THE AUTHOR

JOHN PODHORETZ is the author of the *New York Times* best-seller *Bush Country: How Dubya Became a Great President While Driving Liberals Insane* and *Hell of a Ride: Backstage at the White House Follies 1989–1993*. He is a columnist for the *New York Post*, where he has also been the editorial page editor and television critic, and a political commentator for the Fox News Channel. He was a cofounder of the *Weekly Standard* and has worked at *Time, U.S. News & World Report,* and the *Washington Times*. Podhoretz served as a speechwriter for President Ronald Reagan and as special assistant to drug czar William J. Bennett. He lives in New York City with his wife and daughter.